Fast Bytes

Surfing Anonymously

F. Schaeffer

DATA BECKER®

Published by DATA BECKER CORP
154 Wells Avenue
Newton
MA 02459

Author Florian Schaeffer

Printed in the United States January 2002

UPC CODE 6-80466-90209-6

ISBN # 1-58507-114-5

Important note

The procedures and programs described in this book are given regardless of patent. They are intended for amateur and training purposes only.

All information, technical specifications and programs in this book has been produced by the authors with the utmost care. However, the publishers can provide neither a guarantee, nor accept legal responsibility or any other responsibility, for consequences resulting from incorrect information.

The software and hardware designations and trademarks of companies used in this book shall generally remain subject to the legislation covering trade names, trademarks and protection under patent law.

The text contained in this book are suggestions and examples only. They include selective information only with no claims made for completeness.

In addition, although the text has been created with great care, the publisher and the authors shall accept no responsibility for the completeness or correctness, for the contents of the text or for the success of the users actions after following the information given in this manual. Using the information given in the text is solely at the user's own risk.

The names and addresses given in this text are fictitious. Any resemblance to persons alive or dead is purely coincidental and unintentional.

Preface

Surfing the Net safely - is it actually possible?

As soon as you access the Internet data highway with your computer, security is out of the question. Ultimately, the ideal and secure computer is a system without any contact to the outside world, that is, no disks and CD-drive and no direct contact to other computers by modem or network card.

But this would be a thing of the past as the information society forces the user more and more to communicate with other people, exchange data, and be mobile on a worldwide scale.

Cutting yourself off and closing your eyes is the wrong way to go. You cannot merely inform yourself about weak points and security holes - and there's hardly any subject more current than Internet security as the media constantly reports about new hacker attacks and dangers from the Net. Surfing the World Wide Web is not possible without the user bearing full personal responsibility; and if you don't want your data to be spied on or to be misused by other people, the following security advice certainly helps you to protect your privacy: danger recognized - danger averted.

Despite careful research and utmost topicality, it is hardly possible to prevent the excitement caused by constantly emerging innovations and up-to-date information when dealing with such a highly charged subject area.

In case you come across any pertinent information or cannot find some of the mentioned tools anymore because the Web site has been changed, I would love to hear from you - please send an e-mail to: f.schaeffer@gmx.net.

Have fun reading this book and good luck with the fight against data spies and hackers!

Sincerely,

Florian Schäffer

Contents

1. Immediate measures to ensure your security

Alarm! Hackers are attacking your computer; so before you even make one click on the Web, you should implement the following advice and close risky security holes on your computer. With these immediate measures you make the hacker's life more difficult and protect yourself and your data from unauthorized access as well as other bad surprises. As the hacker attacks against the software giant Microsoft show (compare to page 112), nobody is secure on the Internet - not even such a large company that should particularly be agitated by security.

Make your own decision: Disabling automatic dial-up

Imagine that you have just installed the newest software and - behind your back - the program sends information about you to the software producer afterwards. For convenience, the automatic provider dial-up remains enabled on many PCs. Consequently, each time software is under the impression that it requires an Internet connection, a connection is actually established (for example, because you accidentally clicked a link in the browser). A lot of software has no business being on the Net yet nevertheless likes to establish connections, for instance, to transmit your registration information when installing new software.

If you are using an analog modem, you might still hear the typical dial-up sounds when a connection is established. In the case of ISDN, you are online within seconds.

As a precaution, you should therefore disable the automatic dial-up function and simply put up with the additional effort.

If the option *Connect automatically* has been selected in the dial-up connection dialog window, Internet connections are established without further inquiry.

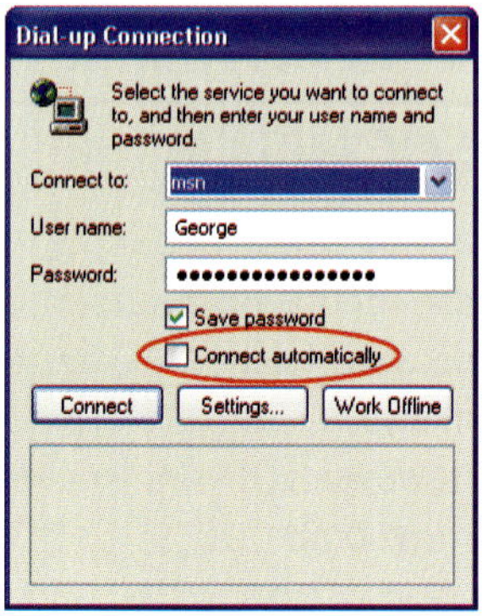

1 To disable the automatic dial-up function, go to *Start/Control Panel/* (*Start/Settings/Control Panel* in 98/ME/2000).

2 Double-click *Internet Options* and select the *Connections* tab in the *Internet Properties* dialog window.

3 Enable the option *Never dial a connection*. Although you must manually dial-up to your provider in the future (for example, by using Dial-Up *Network Connections* under *Start/ Programs/Accessories/Communications*), no expensive Internet connections are established without your knowing about it, and no exchange of data passes unnoticed.

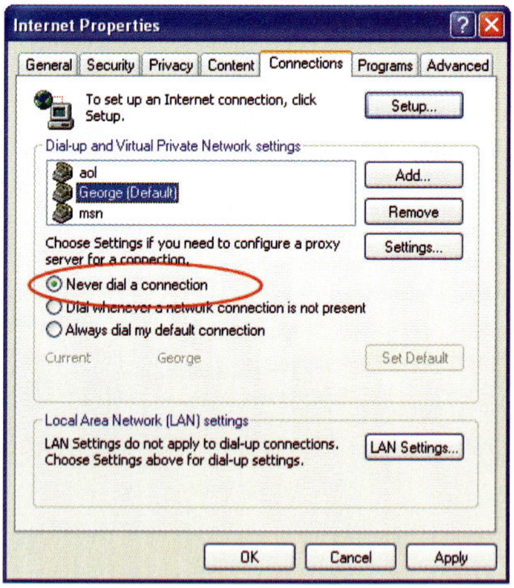

Be aware of Free Internet Dial Up

So you are innocently surfing the Net, and at the end of the month you receive your phone bill asking you to pay a horrendously high amount. After closer inspection of the bill, you might realize that the expensive phone calls were recorded at the same time you were on the Net. How could that happen?

It's simple: Many providers and other suppliers of software CDs that are often attached to magazines and financed by advertising, are establishing new dial-up connections on your PC. These connections are usually established through an expensive telephone number and might cost you more than $1.00 a minute. Most likely, you are asked to confirm the new connection during the installation process; however, it's easy to click *OK* without paying a lot of attention to the actual message box - and before you know it the new provider has set up a new default connection. Each time you access the Internet, the new provider is used, and your telephone bills increase considerably.

1 Open the control panel by going to *Start/Control Panel*; click the *Internet Options* icon.

2 Select the *Connections* tab.

3 Under *Dial-up and Virtual Private Network settings* you can determine which provider has been set to be the *Default* provider. If you think that the wrong provider is selected, choose another one, and click *Set Default* to change the default provider. Alternatively, you can also enable the option *Never dial a connection.* .

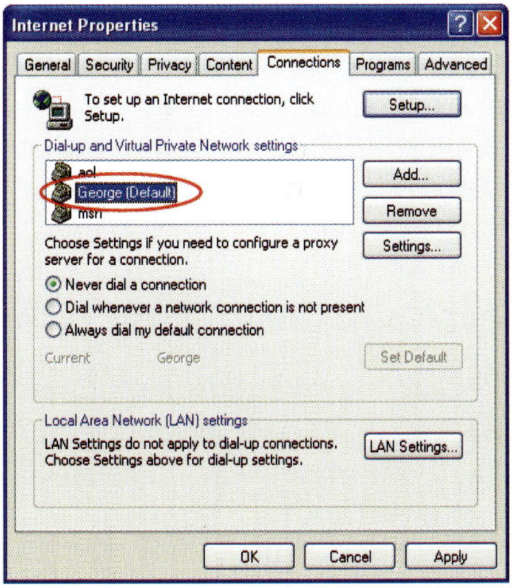

Click *Remove* to get rid of the expensive provider and to avoid getting accidentally caught in the fee trap again.

Deleting provider passwords before someone else gets to them

> **Note**
>
> **Never save passwords**
>
> Saving passwords is convenient and speeds up the dial-up process; however, it also makes the hacker's life easier. Therefore, never save your secret passwords within the software; enter them anew each time instead. No matter where they are, saved passwords are always unsafe as they are a popular target for hackers - particularly when using standard software.

Depending on the application you have installed and the provider used to connect to the Internet, the data is saved at different locations on your PC.

If you did not realize the danger these saved passwords pose up to this point, you can most often delete them from your programs later on - thus making sure that no hacker can access them.

A dial-up network that can save the accessing data, among other things, is almost always used to establish the connection. Some providers offer free software that, on the whole, does not do anything more but create a new dial-up network connection.

1 Passwords and dial-up connections can be deleted conveniently by going to *Start/Control Panel/Internet Options*. Then select the *Connections* tab.

2 Click the corresponding provider listed in the *Dial-up and Virtual Private Network settings* window for which you want to delete an already saved password; then click *Settings*.

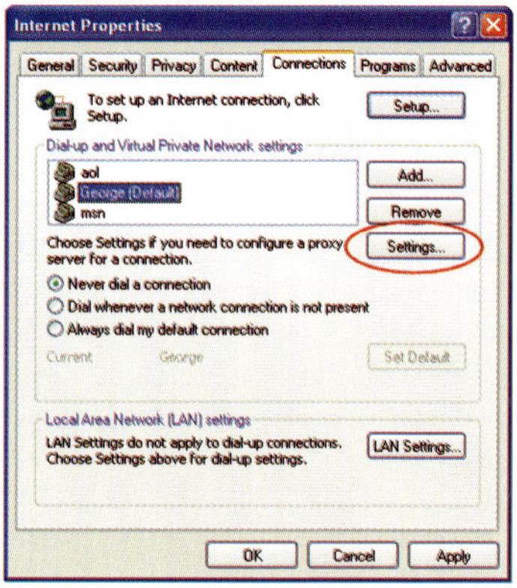

3 Now you can delete the entry displayed in the *Password* data-entry field. If you want to play it safe, you can also delete the *User name*.

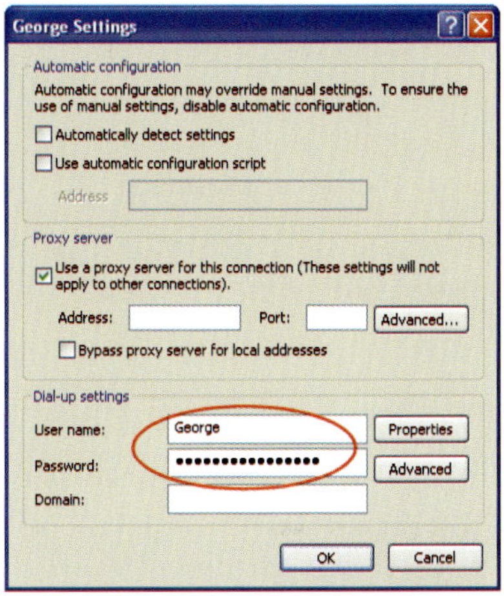

Even if it seems tempting, it's advisable to disable the option for saving the password, unless you are dealing with call-by-call providers.

For most of the call-by-call providers you don't even need a password. Although a user name and password are always requested when entering the dial-up data, you can usually enter any desired text or nothing at all and still access the Net.

Setting security levels correctly in Explorer

Windows – and consequently Internet Explorer as well – use a simple concept to provide more (or less) security when surfing the Net: the zones. Internet Explorer differentiates between the following zones:

- **Internet:** Includes all Web sites that are not contained in any of the following categories.
- **Local intranet:** These are Web sites from the internal network of your company or other local intranets.
- **Trusted sites:** This zone includes certain Web sites that are trusted and must be specified by their address.
- **Restricted sites:** In comparison to the latter category, these Web sites are not trusted, and strict security settings are applied accordingly.

Depending where a Web site is coming from, that is, which zone it is allocated to, particular security settings are applied. These settings can be customized to define the security level for content of particular origin.

The four available security levels are:

- **Low:** Almost everything is allowed and practically no information is passed on to you if questionable activities occur. At this security level almost all doors to your computer are already open for hackers, and your system is hardly protected at all.

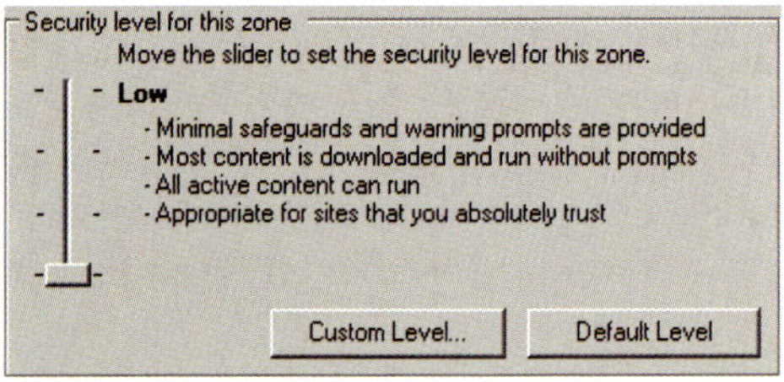

- **Medium-low:** This level offers a little bit more security; however, it is not really secure enough as too many open avenues for hackers still exist. Rarely are you asked by means of a message box if potentially unsafe content should be permitted.

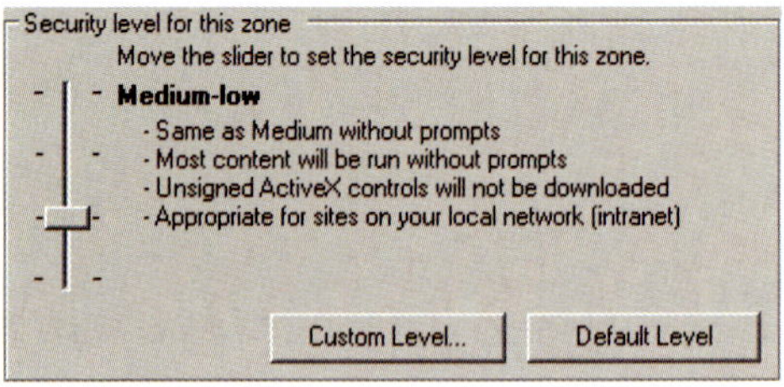

- **Medium:** The happy medium between joyful surfing and a minimum of data security. Microsoft's opinion is that this is the proper setting; however, too many open avenues for real hackers still exist. So if you are interested in taking control of your data and your system, you should not entirely trust this wholehearted promise.

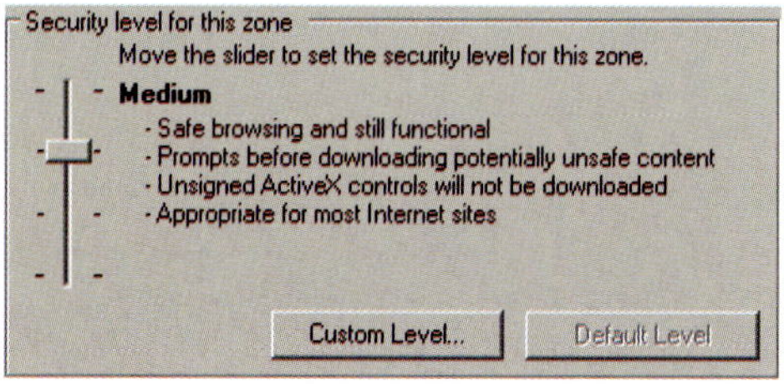

- **High:** Although many Web sites are not displayed at this level, ActiveX (see page 28) is still permitted, and user data is revealed.

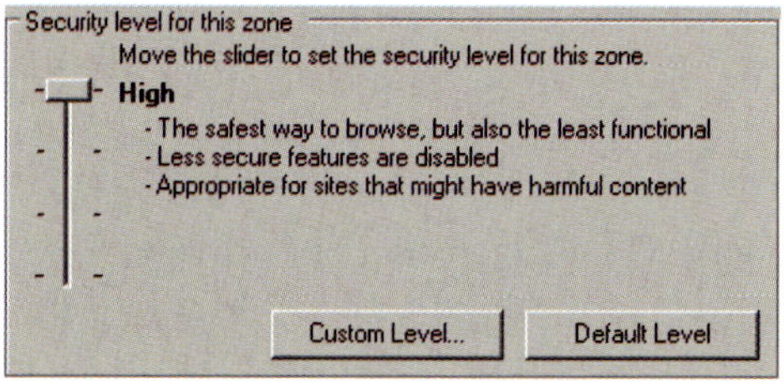

The higher you set the security level of a zone, the fewer unpleasant surprises you have as the rights of different programs and functions are considerably limited. Theoretically, it would therefore always be advisable to select the highest security level to be prepared for any attack. Unfortunately, you would then restrict the Web content to such an extent that many Web sites would simply not be available at all - and surfing the Net would hardly be fun anymore.

Besides, even the highest security level that makes great promises is by far not secure enough. On the contrary, Microsoft still permits far too many unsafe actions. Real security can only be achieved by defining the settings manually. The zone system and the four security levels do, however, offer rudimentary security so that you are somewhat protected when surfing the Net without having to spend time fine-tuning the security settings.

1 Go to *Tools/Internet Options* in Internet Explorer. Optionally, you can also go to *Start/Control Panel/* and select the category *Internet Options*.

Note

Where can I find the Internet Options in Internet Explorer?

Depending on the version of Internet Explorer, you can find the menu item *Internet Options* in the *View* menu or the *Tools* menu.

2 Select the *Internet* globe icon in the top section of the *Security* tab.

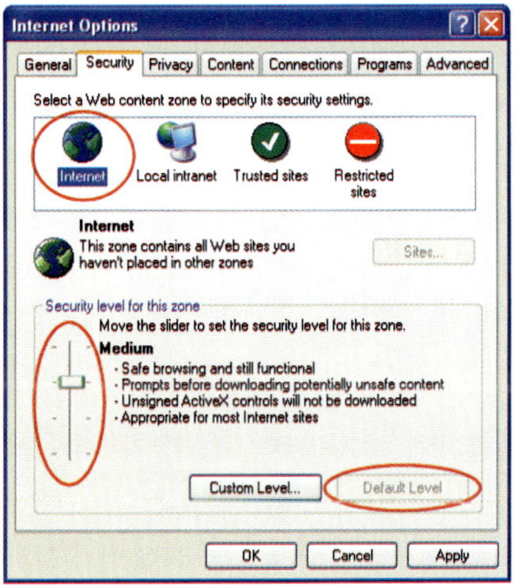

3 You can now use a slider to define the *Security level* for the Internet zone. The lower the slider is set, the more unsafe Internet surfing is as more functions are made accessible. Lower security levels mean having more fun when surfing as most of the Web sites work impeccably; however, it also means a higher security risk. The security level *Medium* is advisable.

Note

Customizing the security level

If you have already manually adjusted a security level at a former point in time to customize the settings (as explained in the chapter about Internet Explorer starting on page 30), you must click *Default Level* first to use the slider. All of your individual settings are lost this way, however.

Security risk Microsoft Office – Protect Microsoft Office – Protect yourself from evil macros

Macros offer innumerable possibilities to facilitate your work, but unfortunately also as many possibilities to destroy your system in which important files are deleted or thousands of e-mails generated and sent out at your expense.

The default settings of MS Office products protect you from macro viruses to a great extent. Often this security measure is disabled because of carelessness, and consequently your computer is particularly at risk.

> **Note**
>
> **What is a macro (virus)?**
>
> Macros are relatively small programs that are embedded in regular documents such as a worksheet or a text document. They are intended to facilitate recurring user tasks. A macro virus abuses this function, and - depending on its version - it can damage or even destroy your system.

Macros are only activated if the corresponding document is opened in an Office application. If a document contains a macro, and you are not sure about it, Office warns you before the contained macro is executed when opening the file. If you don't know the macros (for example, because you received the document as an e-mail), you should disable the embedded macros to avert the risk. This is how MS Office warns you of macros contained in a file to be opened:

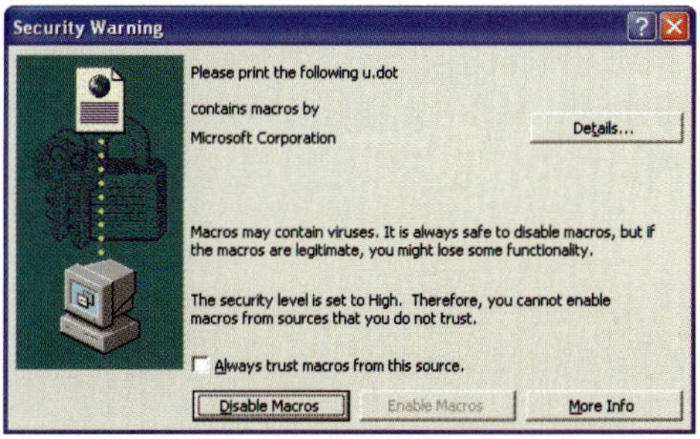

In previous Office versions, this dialog window offered the dangerous option to generally disable macro warnings. If this option is selected, macros are always executed without further inquiry, and a virus can attack your system. Fortunately, this option is somewhat hidden now. In the corresponding dialog window you cannot only permanently enable macros but also check their current settings.

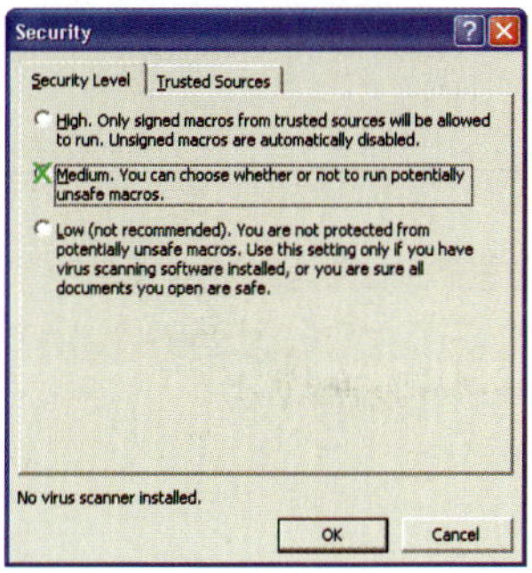

1 Open the *Security* dialog window by going to *Tools/Macro/Security*.

2 Enable the option *Medium* to be warned of macros contained in documents.

3 If you want to play it safe, select the *Trusted Sources* tab and disable the option *Trust all installed add-ins and templates.* This way you are also advised of any macros that you might have already accepted in previous versions to check them. You can enable this option again after the test so that you don't have to confirm each macro every time you start the program.

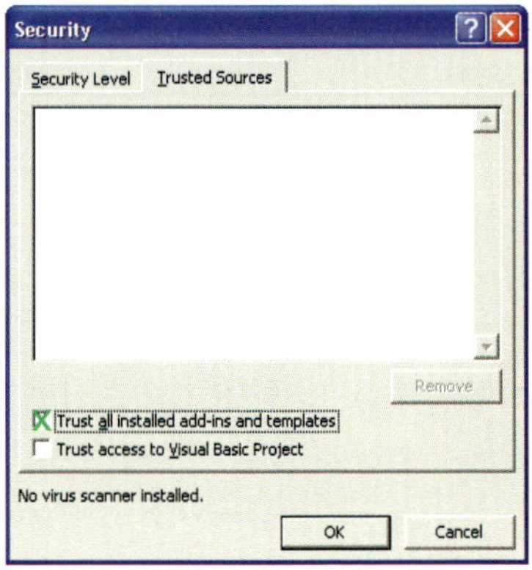

Do you want to call your friends' and colleagues' attention to the risk that macros pose? Then send them a small macro by e-mail. You will be surprised how many recipients open the file and execute the macro without giving it a second thought.

Of course this macro is a "nice" one that does not do any harm on the recipients' computers. The macro used in the following example opens a regular file and displays its content with an added comment. Note how easy it is to create these kinds of macros. It only takes a little bit of criminal inclination to cause real harm; however, because the same way you can read out a file, you can also change or delete one.

Note

It's a small step to criminality

Please note that the following example should only demonstrate the risks that macros pose and is not intended to cause any harm whatsoever. In your own interest, you should not apply your newly acquired knowledge to cause damage to other people. In addition, please select your e-mail recipients carefully as not everybody appreciates this test, and you might get in trouble for it.

To create a macro, you need any desired Microsoft Office product. Although Word is used in this example, the instructions for Excel would be similar, and the risk of executing a macro in the other programs is the same.

1 Start Word and select *Tools/Macro/Macros*.

2 Select the current document from the *Macros in* list box. You can find the corresponding file name in the title bar of the Word window.

3 Enter "AutoOpen" in the *Macro name* data-entry field; then click *Create*.

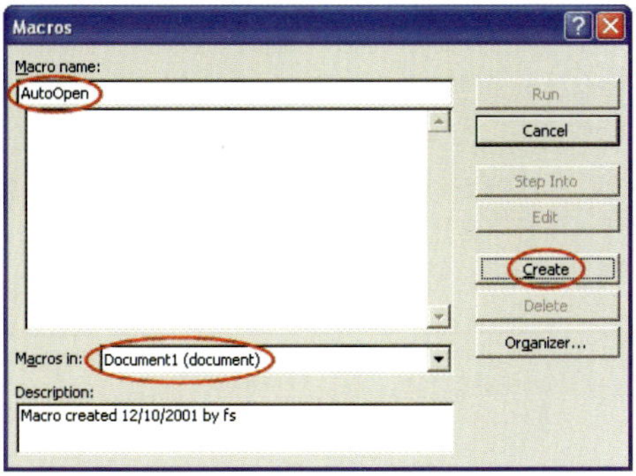

4 The Visual Basic Macro Editor opens displaying a few lines of predefined code. Add the following information to the existing lines and – if you want – delete your name from the green comment line to leave no traces.

```
MsgBox "This is a security demo"
Documents.Open FileName:="c:\autoexec.bat"
```

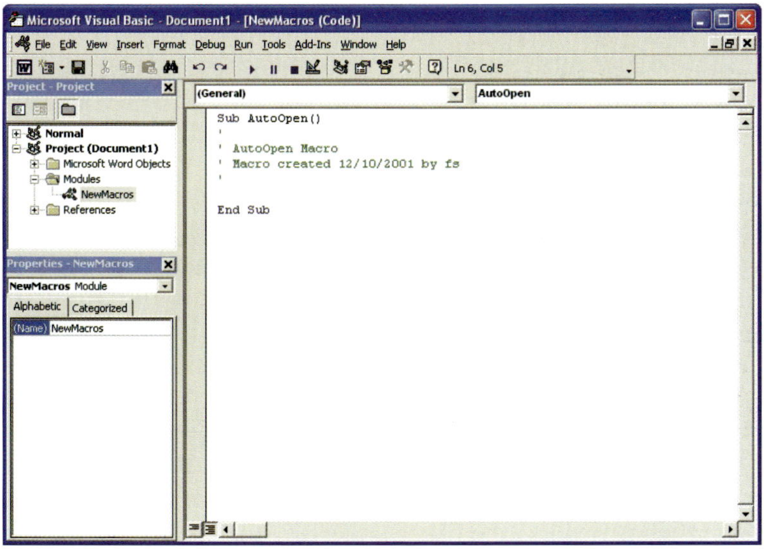

5 Close the Visual Basic-Editor window and save the document under any desired - possibly innocuous - name.

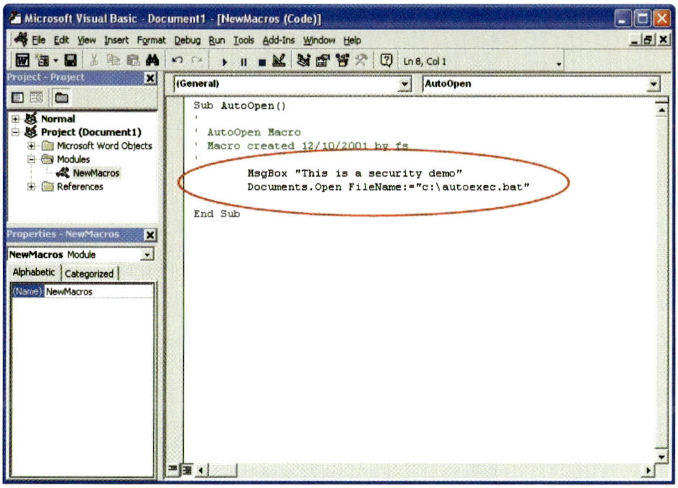

6 Now test the file yourself. To do so, simply open it again in Word.

If you did it correctly and the macro confirmation prompt is enabled on your system, you are asked if you want to execute the macro (see above) - and that's of course exactly what you want.

Thereupon, a message box appears. After clicking *OK*, the content of the file *Autoexec.bat* on C drive is displayed in a new window to demonstrate your power over the system - substituting a really mean action such as deleting the entire hard drive, for instance, which - of course - you would never do.

To raise the awareness of your friends about the risks of macros, send them your Word file containing the macro. Leave the subject line purposely empty and add no further information. Nobody should open a blank e-mail with an attachment without asking you beforehand if the file has actually been sent by you and if it is safe. Any recipient opening the file nevertheless is acting in a grossly negligent manner. You could send them a few security tips a couple of days later (or even better, send this book).

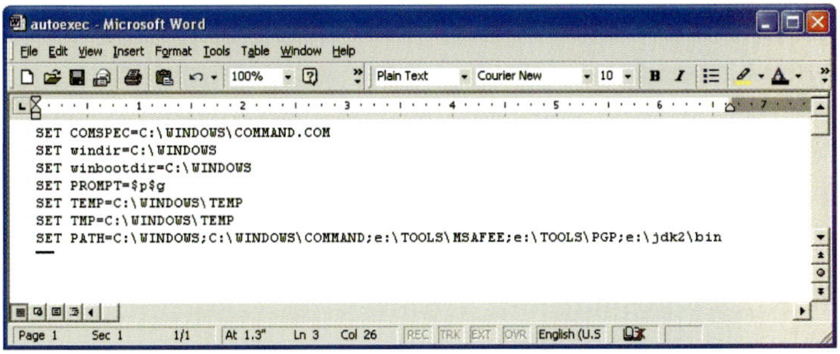

Preventing automatic program start in Outlook

Whereas viruses used to be mainly spread through disks and pirated copies, e-mails have taken over this dubious task in the meantime. Files that are transferred along with e-mails - the attachments - are particularly dangerous. If they are executed directly from the e-mail program, the risk of viruses and similar evil surprises is particularly high.

Such a text document could be opened in Word, for instance, and the contained macros could be executed without further inquiry (compare to page 67).

Outlook and Outlook Express display a paper-clip icon if an e-mail contains an attachment. If you click the attachment, you are usually asked what you would like to do with the attachment: save it first or open it directly.

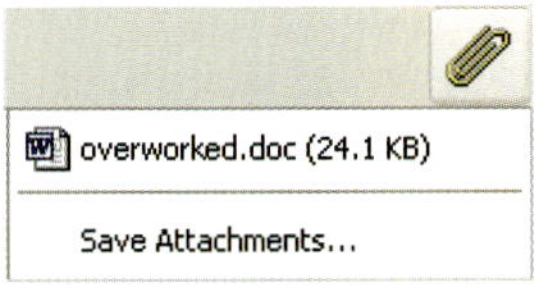

Note

Always save attachments beforehand

It is safer to save any attachments to your hard drive at first and to run them through a virus scanner afterwards (not all virus scanners support the automatic scanning of e-mails). Therefore, Outlook Express always offers the option of saving the attachment.

You can, however, disable the option *Always ask before opening this type of file.* You cannot then be asked in the future if you click a file with the same file extension. Besides, file extensions of Office products can always be trusted according to Microsoft as this particular dialog window never appears when clicking such – a dubious setting considering the frequently recurring virus attacks.

If you have disabled this option in the past and want to have the dialog window displayed in the future, or if you want to activate this function for Office files as well, proceed as follows:

Note

Be aware of the Registry

The following procedure is only intended for experienced users and should be carried out with caution.

1 Start the program by entering the program name "regedit" in the *Run* dialog window.

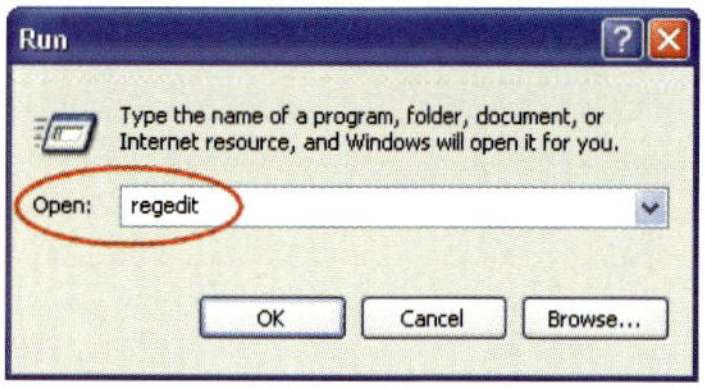

2 Open the key *HKEY_CLASSES_ROOT\.doc*. The last part (*.doc*) is the file extension for Word files. For other file types, look for the corresponding extension.

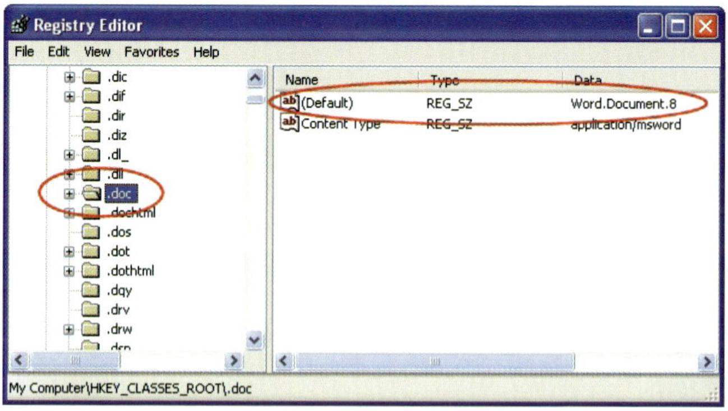

3 Look for the entry to the far right of the (*Default*) entry (here: *Word.Document.8*).

4 Then look for the key with the same name (here: *HKEY_CLASSES_ROOT\Word.Document.8*). Make sure you select the key with the correct spelling because some keys are similar.

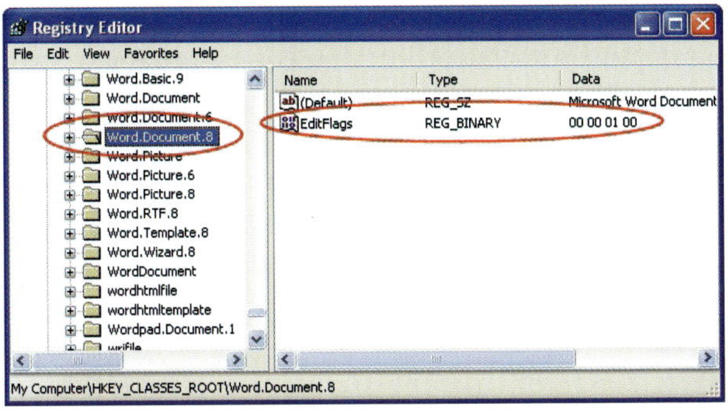

5 Double-click the entry *Edit Flags* in the right section of the window to change the value.

6 Change the third byte to *00*. Disregard the other values.

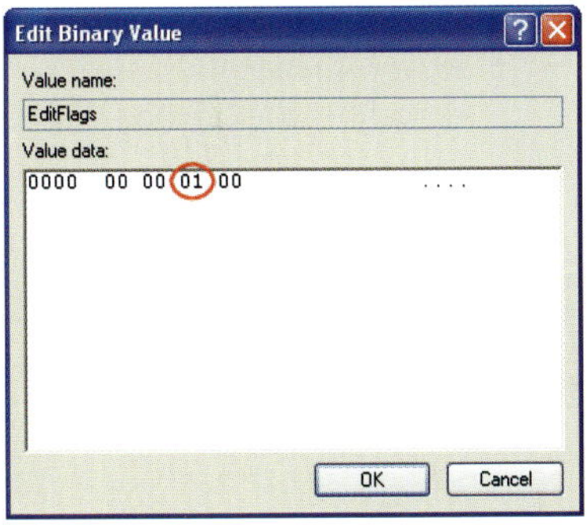

2. The big picture: All of your browser security settings

Current browsers offer a number configuration options, and many of them are intended to make surfing the Net more secure. Only the correct settings - which might take a few mouse-clicks - make your visit on the Internet safe.

The following section helps you to define your settings and leads you through the jungle of technical terms and options. This way you can close all the security holes of your browser, and you understand every available option.

Note

Fun versus security

When defining your security settings, you must always decide for yourself what is more important to you: Fun and multimedia gimmicks or security. Unfortunately, many security settings also limit the usability. A good Web designer acknowledges your demand for security and offers you alternatives. For this reason, the secure settings always take priority here. Should you encounter any difficulties when surfing the Net, you can always change the settings later on, or look for Web pages offering the same or similar content - after all, the Web is full of them!

What's a ... and what are the hidden dangers?

Many security settings are - to the regrets of the surfers - two sided: They are neither good ones nor bad ones, but often they are something in between. Based on your own needs, you must make your own decisions. You are now introduced to important terms so that you can come to your own decision and weigh the security aspects associated with it.

A cookie

A cookie in itself is quite harmless and does not pose any danger to your PC. Your privacy is another story, however, because a cookie can reveal more about you than you would like.

Many Web site operators save small informational bits on your PC - the so-called cookies. The type of data stored in the cookie depends entirely on the supplier of the Web site. Very often it simply records when you visited the particular Web page. To make your future online orders easier, data from form fields, for instance, your address or even your credit card number might be stored. The next time you place an order, the data is already entered in the form - just like magic. It seems like a convenient service, but there is a hidden danger: Imagine someone else reading such a cookie and thus accessing your personal data - or someone else using your computer, placing an order, leaving the suggested credit card number or similar data untouched and only changing the recipient's address.

In addition, the storage of personal data is legally discerning and - in theory - is only allowed upon your approval. A click on *OK* is not sufficient, however, because your personal signature is required for this approval. As it is hardly possible to obtain your signature over the Web, many suppliers act illegally. Theoretically, legal action could therefore be taken against them. As no user seems to be really bothered by it so far, Web site operators cheerfully continue to store your data - and you must make the protection of your personal data your own responsibility.

A company called DoubleClick, for instance, uses another possible application of cookies: They integrated cookies in advertising banners to offer their advertising clients the most detailed information possible. Every time you see such an ad banner, a cookie is saved which records your Web surfing behavior. Because DoubleClick displays over 53 billion (!) banners a month, a gigantic database is created. By combining this data with the data of other companies, it is even possible to obtain the real name and addresses of Web surfers - even if they are not directly known to DoubleClick by their own account.

2. The big picture: All of your browser security settings

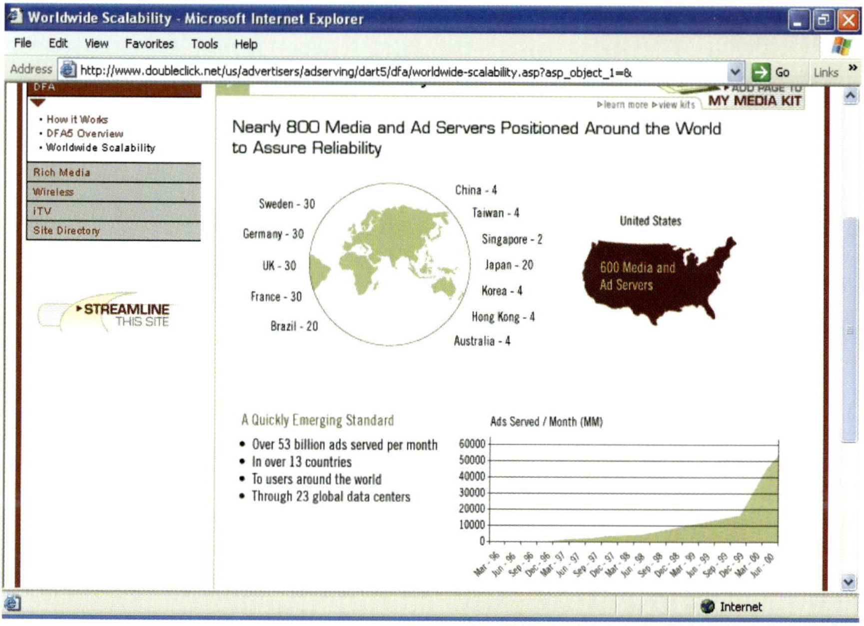

http://www.doubleclick.net/us

Prohibiting cookies from being stored on your computer would be a simple protective measure; unfortunately, many Web hosts wrongfully believe that you cannot avoid cookies and simply shut you out.

Web site hosts are thinking about giving the user - that is, you - the option to decide which ad (or which cookie) you would like to accept (which would be similar to ads sent by e-mail) and to what extent you agree to the tracing of your personal data. This "opt-in" idea is met with a lot of opposition from the industry, however. This comes as no surprise because nobody likes to be spied on, and the number of willing objects would be respectively low. Hence, the economy preaches for the opposite system: opt-out. This means that you are placed on the list of observed (or bombarded with spam) clients first - and only after you explicitly demand to be taken off the list, you are taken off. You must go on the corresponding Web site to find the (usually well hidden) function to be removed from the database.

Note

The expiration date of cookies

Cookies come in two variations: the ones that are permanently stored on your computer, and the ones that are only active as long as you are on the corresponding Web site or as long as the browser is running.

JavaScript

JavaScript can be used to integrate small programs in a Web site that is executed when the Web site is viewed. There are a variety of applications for it such as checking form entries - or the spying out of confidential information.

JavaScript should actually be secure and not allow any destructive actions and attacks; however, news about newly found security holes is always surfacing. Hackers can look at the content of the local hard drive or falsify the address in the browser address line. Visitors are led to believe that they are looking at the site of another supplier while the hacker obtains secret accessing data.

A lot of weaknesses of previous browser versions have already been eliminated, and current browsers should not be so liberal with JavaScript anymore. But these new measures only protect you from flaws that are already discovered and certainly more are out there that have not been discovered yet.

As with cookies, you can also disable JavaScript; however, many Web sites are based on JavaScript and without it, the sites simply won't work.

Java

Java programs, called applets, are programs that are transmitted in addition to a Web site. Java can be used to create games or to display the current stock market prices, for instance.

Note

Security hole in Internet Explorer

Java keeps showing security holes. For instance, a Java program was able to change the security settings in Internet Explorer and to activate ActiveScripting, which provides further opportunities for attacks. (compare to page 30 ff.).

To run a Java applet on your system, you need a virtual machine (VM), which is part of every up-to-date browser. The concept of Java implies that this VM controls the applet's access to the system that is usually highly limited to prevent misuse. The applet runs in a sandbox, and only applications that were classified by the user as being trusted have certain privileges. As usual, exceptions prove the rule, and Java is not really secure. Because the individual browser developers write VMs, they differ from each other respectively; and an entirely secure VM might never exist - to say nothing of the (possibly intentionally) built-in back doors.

Java has relatively few applications such as online banking, for instance, so you can easily disable them without suffering heavy losses.

ActiveX

ActiveX, which is created by Microsoft, can do anything: from helpful gimmicks to destructive attacks - and it is completely redundant.

The user cannot control the mightiness of ActiveX because everything the user can do (accessing files and networks and so forth) a component of ActiveX can do as well. Microsoft actually developed an authenticity procedure in the meantime; however, it is unsatisfactory because too many ActiveX components are accepted due to negligence.

As ActiveX is not available on many (non-Microsoft) systems, a proper Web must do without it (for example, by using Java). Even under Windows, you can therefore easily renounce ActiveX without causing any problems. You should only accept the application of ActiveX if you fully trust a Web site (for example, when doing your online banking) and if you are dealing with a signed ActiveX element.

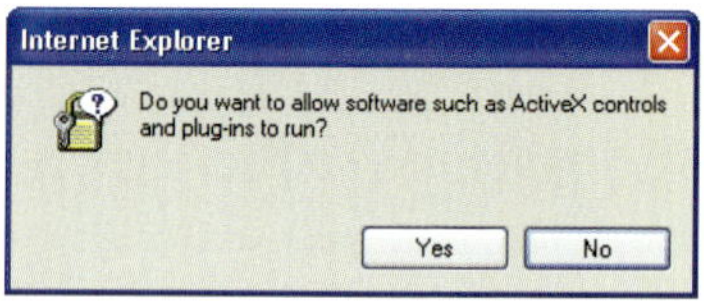

Making Internet Explorer secure

Now that you know about the most important technologies, you can get to work and configure Internet Explorer accordingly. As the default settings are more than questionable, only a little bit of manual work makes Web surfing a secure and fun experience.

Note

The Prompt security option

When defining security settings, you are offered the *Prompt* option often. If you select this option, you are asked if you want to enable or disable the corresponding function for a particular Web site when surfing the Net. By making a decision for each individual Web site, you can keep track of the mechanisms accessing your system. The prompt messages can get annoying after a while, however, if the Web site provider exaggerates and too many prompts must be confirmed.

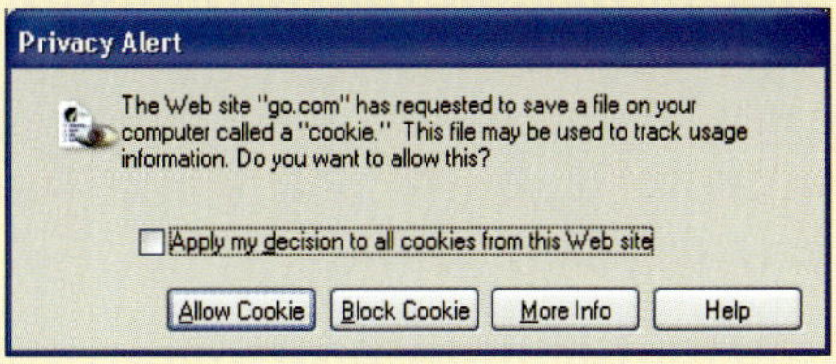

The General settings

This tab doesn't really offer many security settings. Essentially, this tab is about making surfing the Net more convenient; it offers a few basic settings.

1 Open the *Internet Options* dialog window by going to *Start/Settings/Control Panel.* You can also open it directly in Internet Explorer by using the *Tools* or *View* menus.

2 Select the *General* tab.

The *Address* field usually contains the URL of Microsoft so that each time you start Internet Explorer, Microsoft's Web site is displayed. This in itself is not really a security risk; however, it does take up time and money and simply helps Microsoft to control the distribution of its browsers.

You are better off entering a really interesting Web site that you like visiting. You can also click *Use Blank*; the address field then displays the terms *about:blank* and no Web site is opened automatically.

Customized security settings

Now we are getting down to business. The zone concept of Internet Explorer was already introduced in the chapter about immediate measures at the beginning of the book (starting on page 13). As the simple security levels hardly provide adequate protection, all relevant settings should be adjusted manually. This way you can decide for yourself what is more important to you: surfing with convenience or the security of your data.

It is annoying that Microsoft does not deem it necessary to explain the settings' effects and all of the following options in detail. Neither the Help function nor the Internet provides satisfactory results. This means that no detailed description is available for a number of settings, and only recommendations, which have been considered useful by different users, can be made. This fact gives many security conscious users the creeps because you can only decide in favor of a setting if you know the consequences.

1 Select the *Security* tab.

2 Select the *Internet* zone and click *Custom Level* to customize your security settings.

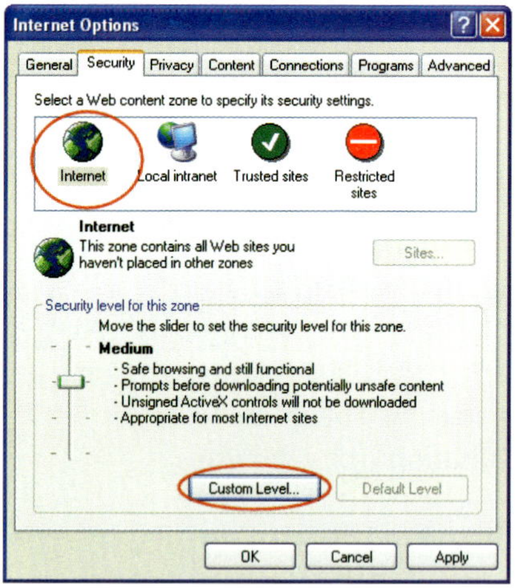

ActiveX isn't a necessity

As ActiveX is generally not very secure, you should disable it entirely or select the prompt option so you can make individual decisions based on the Web site host at the time. Once in a while you might miss out on a few Web site gimmicks this way;

however, this loss is easily compensated by the security you gain. And you won't miss out on the really important things because the Web site host is most likely trying to sell you something. Consequently, the company looks after every visitor – even the ones not using the ActiveX function. If not, look for an alternative supplier; you can find ample on the Web. On page 108, Comet Cursors are introduced to demonstrate how your system can be bombarded with ActiveX and why you must be careful when dealing with ActiveX.

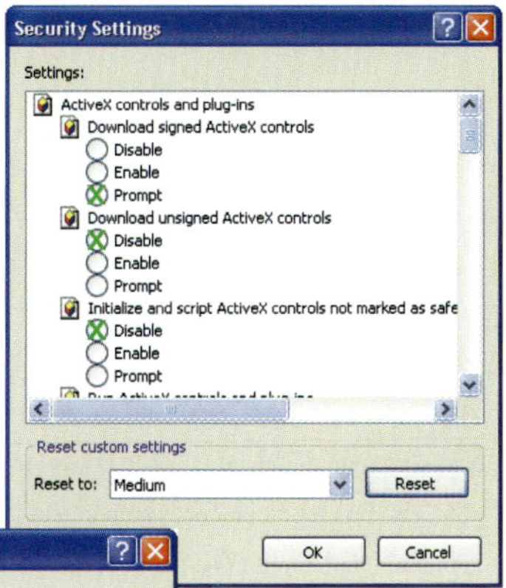

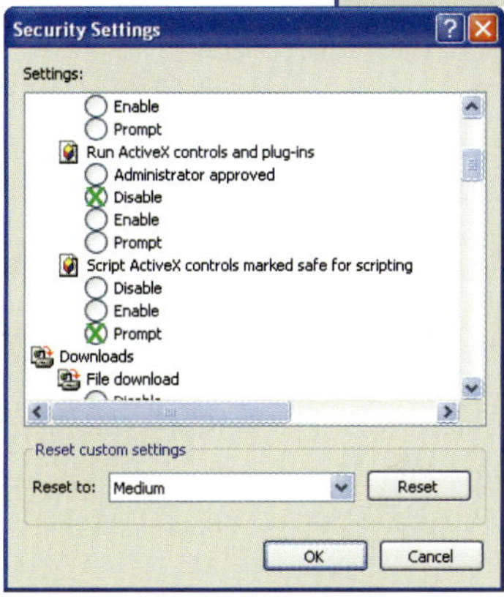

Option	Setting
Script ActiveX controls marked safe for scripting.	Prompt
Initialize and script ActiveX controls not marked as safe	Disable
Run ActiveX controls and plug-ins	Prompt
Download signed ActiveX controls	Prompt
Download unsigned ActiveX controls	Disable

Using the User Authentication to disclose your identity

The *User Authentication* setting controls the way you log on to servers that require your authentication. This authentication is usually encountered with FTPs, where you usually log on anonymously. If the FTP host allows you to download an image from the server, your browser reveals your e-mail address, which can then be misused. If you select the option *Prompt for user name and password*, you are asked to register at which point you can decide which data you want to reveal.

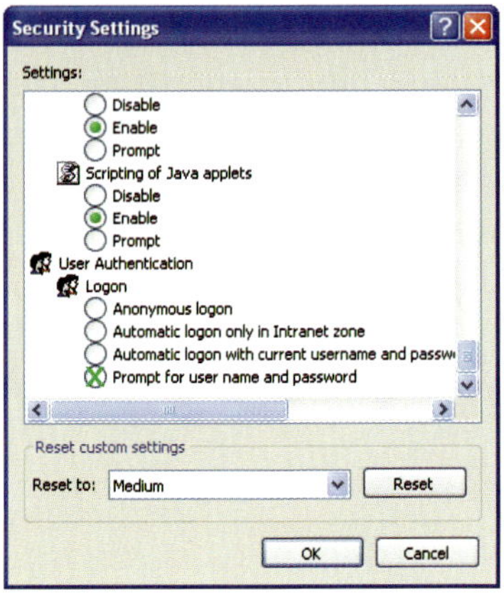

Note

Anonymous FTP registration

When registering with an anonymous FTP server, it is good form to enter the term *anonymous* in the user name field and your e-mail address in the password field. Because this practice is often abused to obtain your address, you should forgo the convenient settings and enter the data yourself, if required, if you are sure that you are dealing with a public FTP server and that you won't be simply spied out.

Downloading files from the Web

Downloading files (*File download* setting) is usually not dangerous, and without it you cannot obtain new updates or software from the WWW. You should scan the downloaded file for viruses afterwards, however.

Download fonts only if the Web designer thinks that the site requires a particular font to display the Web site optimally. You can do without this particular font most of the time. Although, you might not see the Web site in its intended splendor, you won't miss out on its content.

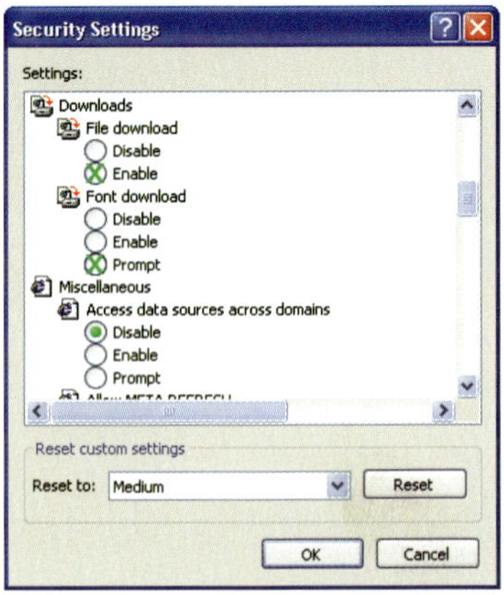

Option	Setting
File download	Enable
Font download	Prompt

Java applets make the Web more diverse

Under *Java permissions* you should select the option *High safety* or *Disable Java*, which is even safer. The less authority the applet has, the lower the risk of your computer being negatively affected. If you don't need Java for online banking or similar tasks, you can disable it entirely. If you open a Web site that needs Java without fail, you are advised and can enable Java at that point in time.

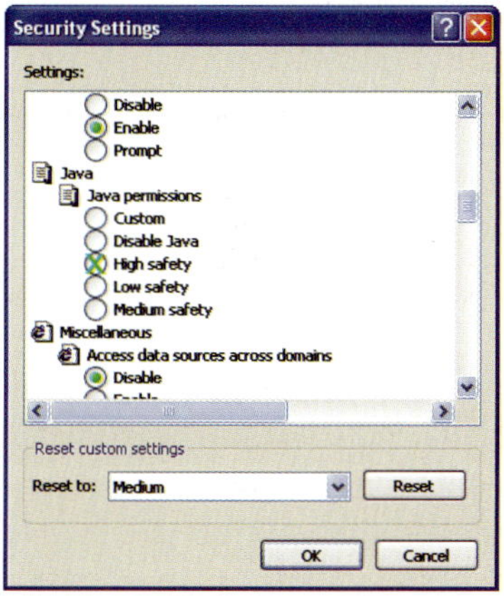

Be careful with JavaScript and VBScript

Unfortunately, Microsoft does not distinguish between JavaScript and VisualBasicScript (VBScript). Although JavaScript poses its own dangers, one can hardly advise users to disable it because hardly any Web site isn't using it nowadays. VBScript, however, is hardly needed by anybody on the Web, and it would be useful if a separate option to disable it existed.

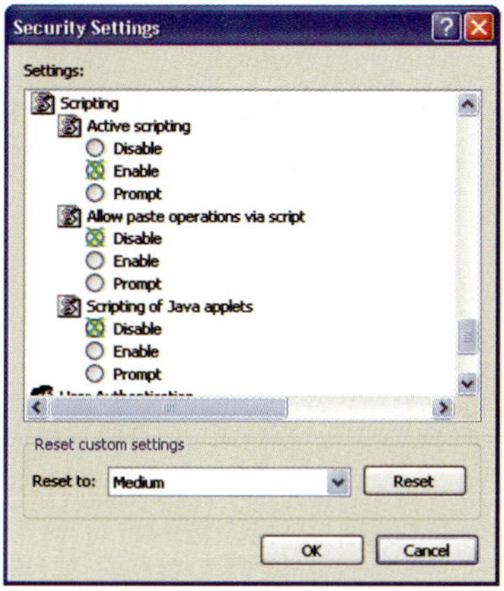

If the option *Allow paste operations via script* is enabled, the content of your Clipboard - to which you might have just copied private information from other applications - can be read by Java Script programs (see page 27). Java applets can also execute JavaScript code, which is not always desired. Therefore, you can disable the corresponding option.

Option	Setting
Active scripting	Enable (better: Prompt)
Allow paste operations via script	Disable
Scripting of Java applets	Disable

Note

Avoiding ActiveScripting

ActiveScripting can generally not be disabled in the local security zone. You should therefore be particularly careful with local Web sites as a saved Web site has free reign, putting your system in danger.

Miscellaneous settings

The category *Miscellaneous* summarizes additional options that did not fit into any other category: *Access data sources across domains* means that a Web site is allowed to access files from another server, that is, not only from the one it is saved on. This function can disguise the origin of Web sites; therefore, you should select the *Prompt* option to keep things under control. This way you are informed if different servers are accessed, and you can agree or reject (rather rarely) this access if you feel like a hacker might be at work.

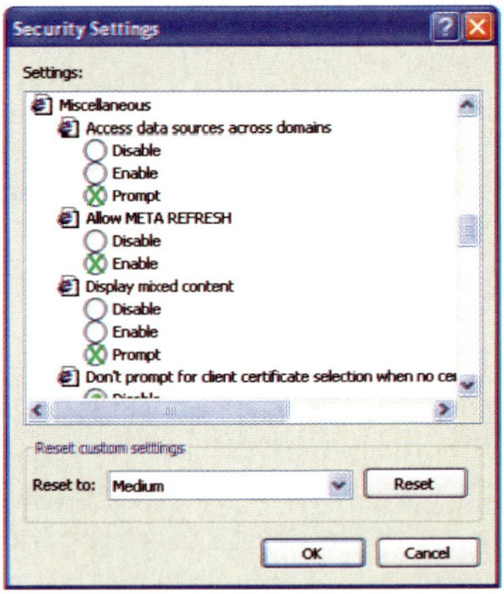

Numerous suppliers would like to install programs on your desktop that, of course, should be avoided. Otherwise, it might not take long until you have a fair amount of programs installed that you actually didn't want in the first place. You can always create a desktop shortcut by yourself after you download a program as usual and install it manually.

IFRAMEs are HTML design tools that allow you to define certain window sections in which additional Web content such as other Web sites, for instance, can be displayed. It is easy to loose track of the Web site's origin this way, though, and you take an unnecessary risk.

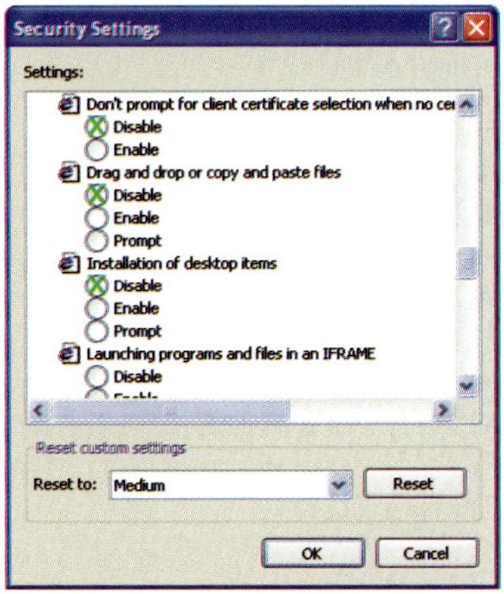

You should only allow frame sets that display different Web sites (of different domains) in a number of frames (and therefore hide the site's origin) in exceptional cases. Most of the Web sites work without frames because Netscape does not support them.

Any data entered in form fields is usually non-encrypted, which basically poses a certain risk as the entry is transmitted as uncoded text over the Internet. Considering the many non-encrypted forms you must fill in, you cannot avoid this risk, however.

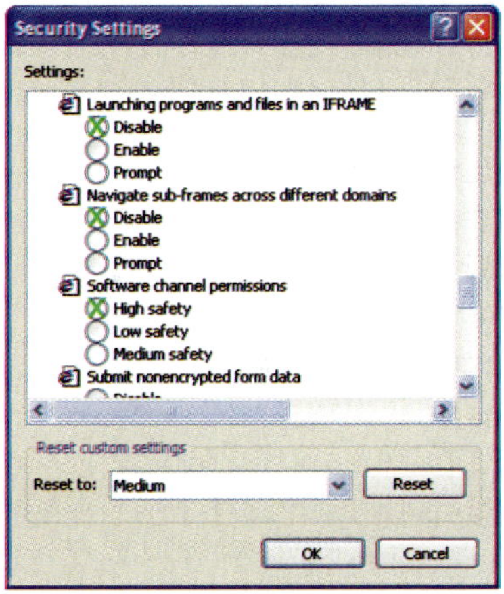

If you have signed up with any software channels, it is possible to transfer programs to your computer that, in turn, can be contaminated with viruses. To ensure that these channels do not have too much access, drastically limit the *Software channel permissions*. You hardly miss out on anything.

Option	**Setting**
Access data sources across domains	Prompt
Installation of desktop icons	Disable
Launching programs and files in an IFRAME	Disable
Navigate sub-frames across different domains	Disable
Submit non-encrypted form data	Prompt
Software channel permissions	High Security

2. The big picture: All of your browser security settings

Now that you have defined the security settings for the *Internet* zone, you can proceed with the remaining zones in a similar fashion.

1 Click *Local intranet* to define its security settings.

2 As you did for the *Internet* zone, you can now click *Custom Level* again to define all options for any Intranet Web sites (that is if you actually have access to a business intranet).

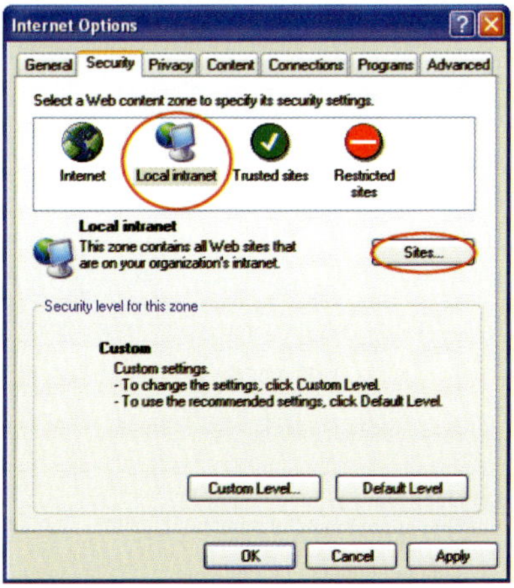

3 If you want to save yourself the effort, you can click *Sites* to define the Web sites to be included in the local intranet zone. If you disable all options in the next dialog window, all intranet sites are treated the same way as *Internet* sites.

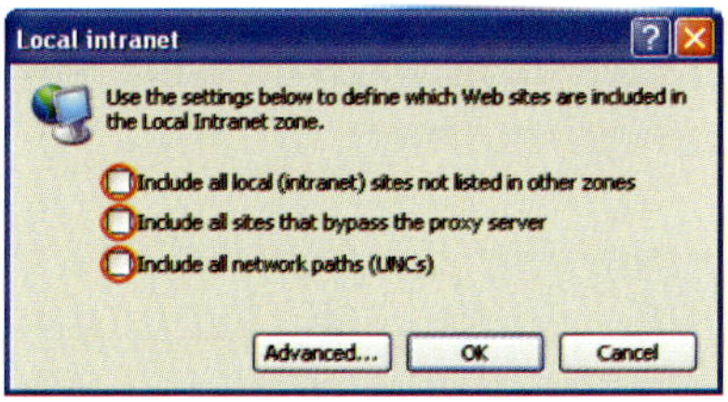

4 The security settings for the *Trusted sites* zone must be defined as well. You only have to do this, however, if you have classified any sites as trustworthy in the corresponding dialog window by clicking *Sites*. You can add any Web sites if you assume they cannot damage your data, for instance, to this zone. Web sites not listed are treated according to the security settings of the *Internet* zone.

5 To configure the *Restricted sites* zone, proceed the same way as with the previous step.

The only difference is that you should now list the Web sites that you don't trust by clicking *Sites*. These sites are then treated under extremely high security settings.

The cookie monster's favorite: Cookies

Permanent and temporary cookies can be treated differently. You can confidently view permanent cookies as a nuisance and refuse to accept them. Many online stores require you to accept temporary cookies, as without them, you might not be able to buy anything (unless it is a really well-designed store). As temporary cookies do not leave any permanent traces behind, not too many bad things can be said about these bits of information. In case of doubt, the Web site host can advise you that cookies are absolutely necessary to access a particular site, and you can always decide at that point in time whether you want to accept the cookie or not.

Click the *Privacy* tab to find the required settings. Use the slider to roughly define the settings. Click *Advanced*, to define the settings in detail:

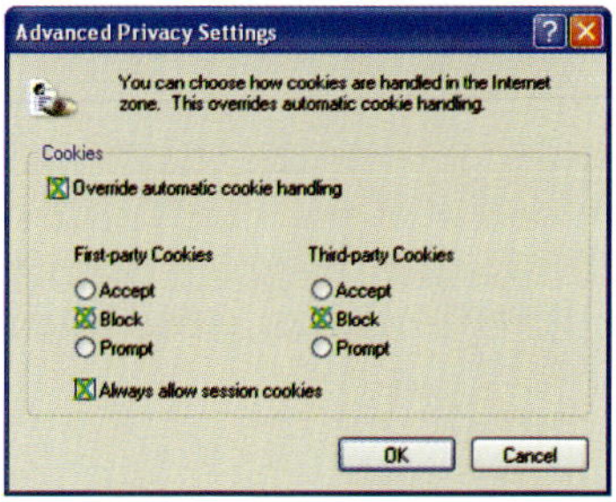

Option	Setting
First-party Cookies	Block
Third-party Cookies	Block
Always allow session cookies	Enable

Using the Content Advisor to block Web sites

Do you want to censor Web sites and protect your children from criminal sites or other Web sites that might put minors at risk? Then you are in the right place! Internet Explorer already provides the suitable functions, and no major configurations are required to block any questionable sites. Compared to other commercial programs that offer fewer features, this is a useful function. However, it does not supercede your children's education; it offers a certain amount of control.

Note

Censoring content equals the protection of minors?

Although rating software such as the one provided by Internet Explorer offers a certain amount of protection, a computer magazine reported that 3% of minors are able to evade censoring software or to defy control entirely by simply not surfing at home.

1 The *Content* tab contains a number of configurable options to control the content of a Web site. Microsoft offers a censoring function to block undesired Web sites. You can define conditions for accessing Web sites, for instance, to protect your children from Web sites that might put them at risk. Click *Settings* to customize the Advisor. If you are using the Content Advisor for the first time, you must click *Enable* first to activate it.

A message box appears advising you that you are not allowed to see a Web site due to the rating settings (embarrassingly it is the site of the ratings' supplier who classified his own Web pages incorrectly).

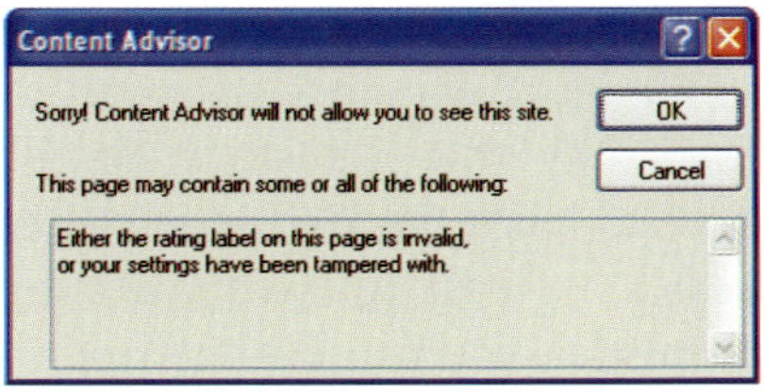

Note

This is how the censoring works

By default, Internet Explorer uses the **R**ecreational **S**oftware **A**dvisory **C**ouncil (RSACi) Rating System of the **I**nternet **C**ontent **R**ating **A**ssociation (ICRA). This rating system classifies Web sites into different categories such as sex, nudity, or violence. The Web site host voluntarily provides information about his Web site; a hidden label is integrated in the Web site that can be evaluated by the browser. There's only one problem: numerous possible loopholes. Web site hosts can integrate incorrect references; consequently, Web sites with an innocent-looking domain name might be displayed – no matter what their content looks like. In addition, relatively few Web site hosts undergo this procedure because numerous others are available.

2 On the *Ratings* tab, select the category whose rating level should be defined. Use the slider to set the desired *Level*. The higher the level, the more content is allowed, and the more Web pages are displayed.

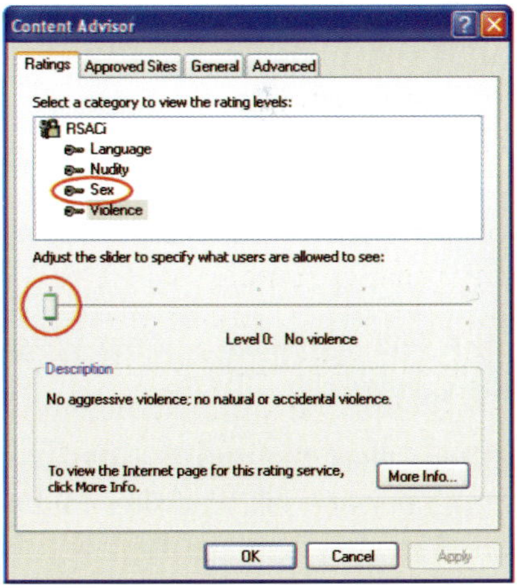

3 Because many Web site hosts do not take part in the RSACi Rating System, you cannot view their Web sites when activating the filter - no matter how harmless the Web site's content (for example, search engines). To avoid the ratings for individual Web sites, you can use the *Approved Sites* tab to create a list of always viewable or never viewable Web sites. To do so, enter the entire URL in the data-entry field and click *Always* to approve a Web site or *Never* to block a site.

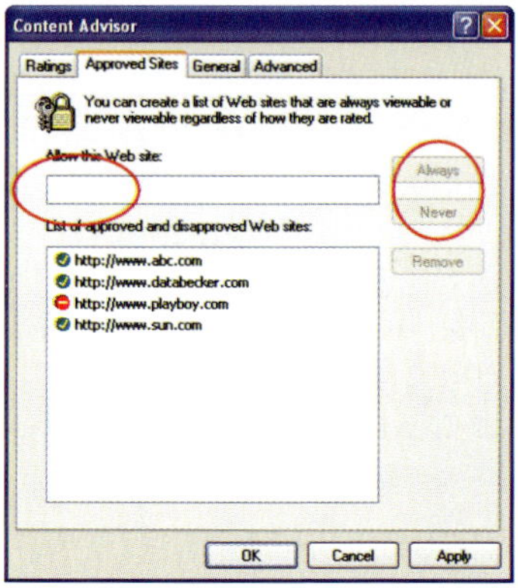

The desired Web site does not contain a rating and is therefore not displayed.

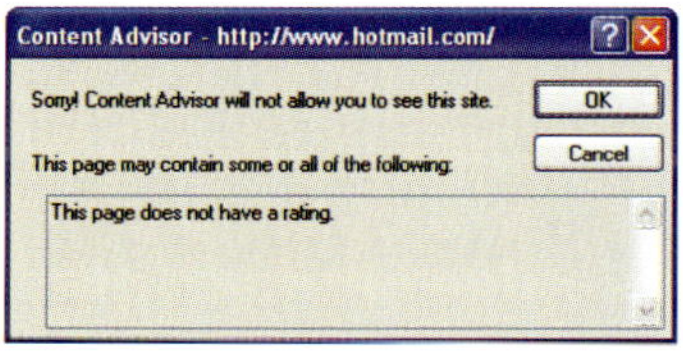

Note

Recorded Web sites

The list displays Web sites for which you have defined your own rules. To delete an entry, select it and click *Remove*. While you are surfing the Net, you are asked (depending on the settings explained below) if you want to unblock a currently blocked Web site. This site is then automatically added to the list. Please note that entire "Web sites" is unblocked and blocked. If you approve the Web site http://www.abc.com, for instance, all Web pages containing this domain name are approved.

4 A few additional settings were summarized in the *General* tab.

If you select the option *Users can see sites that have no rating*, all Web sites that are not rated by the Rating System are displayed. Because this applies to almost all Web sites, the rating system is virtually nullified this way.

5 If you select the option *Supervisor can type a password*, you can unblock a blocked Web site by entering a password. The password can be entered or changed by clicking *Create Password*. When you finish your rating levels by clicking *OK*, you are asked to enter a password at the latest. A password has to be entered to activate the rating settings; otherwise, the settings could simply be modified by anybody.

By entering the password, the censored Web site can be displayed or you can specify, if the entire site or individual pages should be added to the list of approved Web sites (see above).

Note

Password loopholes

What would a book about security be without the tricks on how to get around this pseudo-security - because sooner or later, you and especially your kids find out about them anyway. The password protection and consequently the entire rating system have one huge problem: Because the password is your only protection, there is, more or less, no protection at all. You can go into the Registry and delete the entry *Key* from the *HKEY_LOCAL_MACHINE\Software\Microsoft\Windows\CurrentVersion\Policies\Ratings* key. Once you restart the browser, a new password can be created or the rating system can simply be left disabled.

6 If you click *Find Rating Systems*, you are linked to a Microsoft Web site letting you know that additional rating systems are available that can be installed on your computer. The Web site http://www.safesurf.com/iesetup, for instance, offers an additional rating system and also explains how to use it.

Certificates provide information about the Web site host

Certificates are intended to confirm the authenticity of suppliers of Web content and to make the data transfer over the Net more secure by allowing you to screen the partner you are currently exchanging data with and to verify his trustworthiness.

1 You should start your housekeeping now and simply delete all of your certificates to tidy up your collection of certificates and to eliminate the ones that you have accepted due to negligence. Certificates that might be needed again, for example, for banking, can always be accepted later on. Click *Certificates* to open the following dialog window.

2 Select the entry *<All>* from the *Intended purpose* list box.

3 Select the first tab called *Personal* and highlight all certificates (click the first list item, press the Shift key, and then click the last list item).

4 Click *Remove* to delete all certificates. Confirm any possible prompts to delete the certificates.

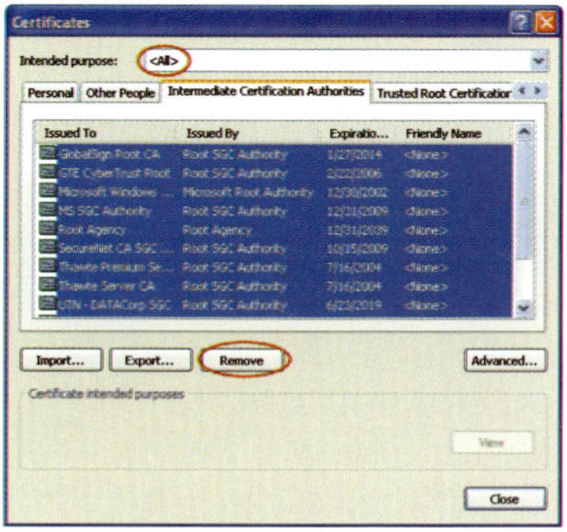

5 Proceed the same way with the certificates of the other tabs. Deleting the *Intermediate Certification Authorities* can be a problem, however, as the browser cannot differentiate between genuine and self-generated certification anymore.

6 Close this dialog window again; click *Publishers* in the *Internet Options* dialog window.

7 Select all publishers and click *Remove*.

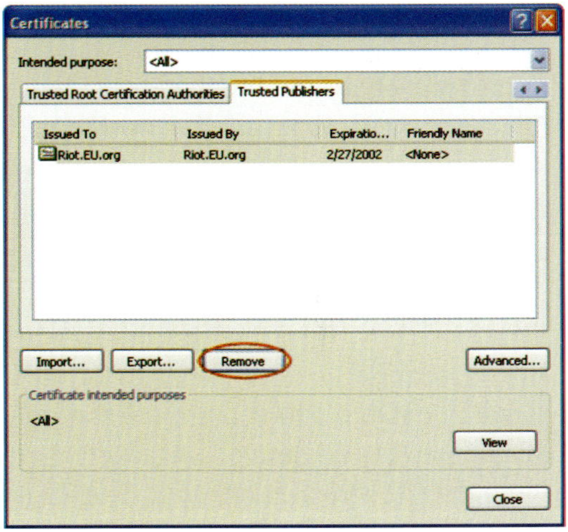

This is where personal information about you is collected

In addition, you can view your stored personal information, correct it if desired or delete it entirely to avoid revealing too much about yourself.

As with many other programs, Internet Explorer seems to be willing to provide information. Of course, this always happens under the disguise of making the user's life easier and more convenient - the catch phrase is "user-friendliness". Hidden dangers lurk behind this user-friendliness far too often, however, that can be used against you in no time. Although it is convenient that you don't have to remember your passwords, for instance, doesn't user-friendliness go a little bit too far in this case? Why have passwords in the first place if any user can plunder your bank account by simply entering a character?

The AutoComplete function suggests previous entries ...

... and might even enter the password if necessary.

Internet Explorer 5 offers a dubious data-entry tool: any data entered in form fields is saved. If the Web site is opened again, the data is automatically entered again as soon as the initial character is entered in the form field. Without question, this feature saves time – especially for the stranger who doesn't have to waste time guessing your personal data. That passwords are entered automatically is particularly worrisome.

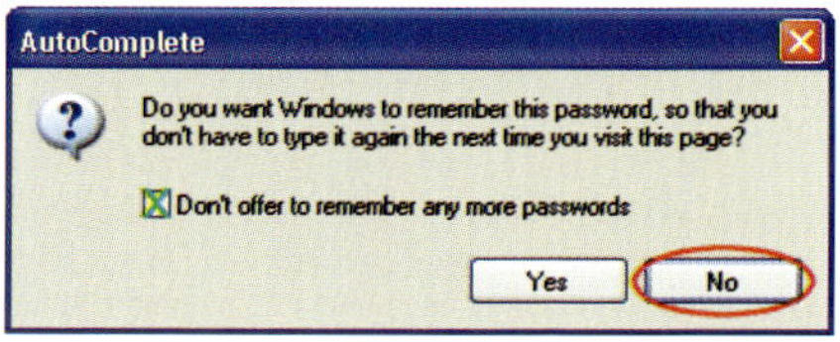

There is only one answer to a question like this one: *No* for now and also in the future.

This mechanism is risky because it is activated by default, and you are unknowingly saving the entered data on your hard drive. Although the saved information is encoded, it does not prevent an experienced hacker from cracking the code. As soon as he has your file, he can misuse all of your passwords, because the suitable Web site to which the data applies has to be saved in addition to the access information.

1 The required settings can be found by clicking *AutoComplete* on the *Content* tab.

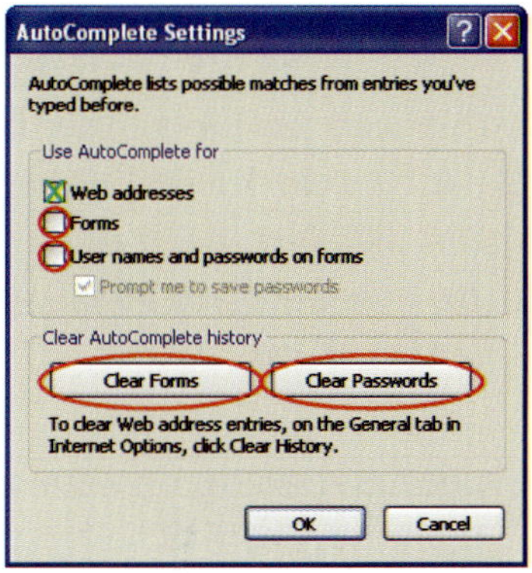

2 Disabling the AutoComplete function for *User names and passwords on forms* is the safest option. Only the option *Web addresses* can be left activated.

3 To make sure that no previously existing data is being saved, click the *Clear Forms* and *Clear Passwords* .

4 Back in the *Internet Options* dialog window, click *My Profile* to find out which personal information already exists about you.

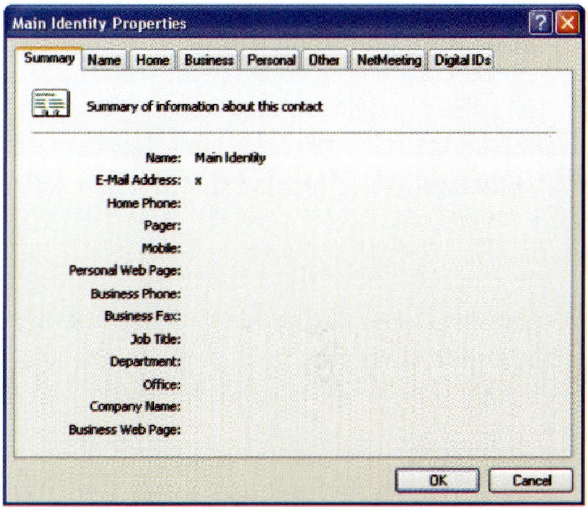

5 All data that was entered on various tabs might be used for NetMeeting, among other things, and sent to other users which - to say the least - have no business knowing your personal information. Therefore, you should rigorously delete all tab entries.

More security settings

The security settings of Internet Explorer are somewhat scattered. The following settings apply at any time, for instance, and do not depend on the zone model that is used for other security aspects. This is not insightful, for these options considerably aid in protecting your information from the eyes of other Internet users after all.

Apart from the display options, additional security settings appear on the *Advanced* tab.

2. The big picture: All of your browser security settings

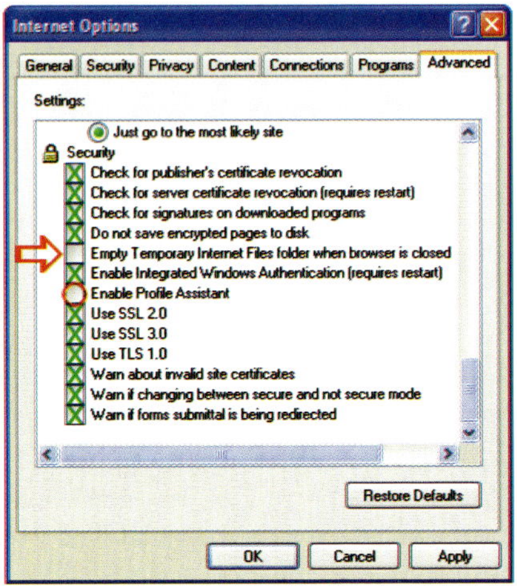

- *Check for server certificate revocation* checks whether a certificate is still valid. Although this takes some time when surfing the Net, it increases the security and does no harm in any way.
- The same applies for *Check for publisher's certificate revocation*.
- If the option *Warn about invalid site certificates* is selected, a warning is displayed to advise you about Web site hosts presenting a wrong or invalid certificate.
- The option *Warn if changing between secure and not secure mode* ensures that you don't switch from safe to unsafe sites by mistake. A brief warning is displayed that might be a bit annoying; however, it prevents your from being under the misconception of feeling safe.
- Internet Explorer saves all of the viewed Web sites in a temporary file (see also the chapter about data traces starting on page 126), which can be accessed by other PC users. If you delete this data, and you open the same Web site again, the entire data has to be transferred again instead of being read in from the cache - which can lead to delays.
- *PCT 1.0*, *SSL 2.0*, *SSL 3.0* and *TSL 1.0* are different encoding procedures that should be enabled to ensure that they are available if required.
- The *Profile Assistant* spies out your saved profile data for Web site hosts (see above) and is hardly used by any Web site. You can therefore leave it disabled.
- You should not simply save Web sites containing confidential information as other security settings might then apply for the Web site, and anybody having access to your computer could view the files. To prevent this from happening, you should enable the option *Do not save encrypted pages to disk*.
- If form data is not sent to the server that requested it, select the option *Warn if forms submittal is being redirected* to be warned about it.

Known security holes of browsers

Regardless of which browser you choose, one thing is certain: a completely secure browser does not exist. Some kind of security hole always exists, and blindly trusting the advertising pitches made by the manufacturer is the wrong approach to the problem.

If you want to prevent unknown people from hacking into your system by forcing their way in through backdoors, you must always be on guard. It is not enough to simply install the latest browser versions; you should also go directly to the manufacturer and its recommended sites to inform yourself about the most recently discovered weak points - current versions especially often suffer from the latest child sicknesses, so you should keep your eyes carefully open.

Do a browser check

To discover security risks in your browser, go to one of the several Web sites that locate your browser's weak points and give you tips on how you can remedy them, so they don't offer hackers any possibilities for attack. In addition, you can always find the latest information about the newest discoveries on the Internet.

If you are always waiting to read about the latest dangers in computer magazines, you are always too late. By the time a relevant article appears in a monthly magazine, the hackers have already been informed and use the short span of time to take advantage of the weak points. You can always find current reports and, more importantly, also the solutions on the Net.

http://www.guninski.com/index.html

2. The big picture: All of your browser security settings

This is how the Bulgarian Georgi Guninski has made a name for himself internationally as a detective of security holes. On his Web site, http://www.guninski.com/index.html, you can arguably find the latest security information.

The site demonstrates how many bugs work and what effect the errors have, and also gives relevant tips for eliminating them. It would be best to actually try out one or two of the shortcomings, for only then can you believe how simple it really is to get at information or to use the browser against you.

The following example shows an actual virus that used a security hole in mid November 2000 that was already known for half a year. Cynical people could say that, if you have neglected to think about your browser's security within this time period, you should be harmed.

The e-mail worm "Blebla" uses Outlook and Internet Explorer's weak points, in a similar manner to Melissa (see page 56). As a new twist, however, it does so without the user executing a specific file by double-clicking it or something similar. Instead, it uses Microsoft's self-developed IFRAME and ActiveScripting.

1 Go to Guninski's Web site and switch to the category for your browser. Because Blebla only affects Internet Explorer and Outlook, switch to the *Internet Explorer* category.

2 The list is in chronological order, with the newest discoveries at the beginning. To inform yourself about the risks of the mechanism used by Blebla, you must find the *IFRAME* reference.

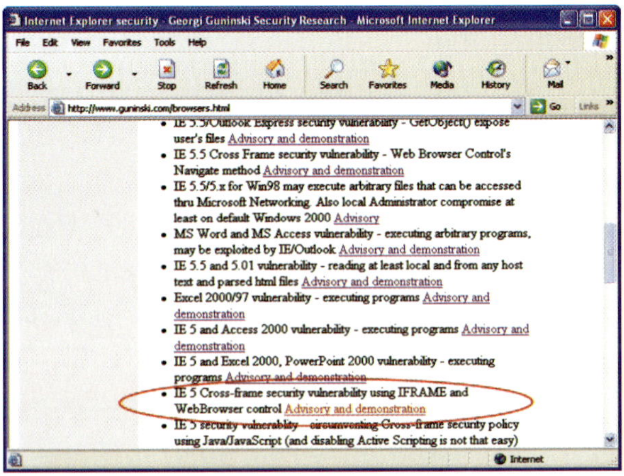

3 At the end of the detailed description of the problem, you find a solution (if available) for plugging the security hole: either through an update of the software or by working around it, which, although it doesn't solve the problem, averts the danger just the same.

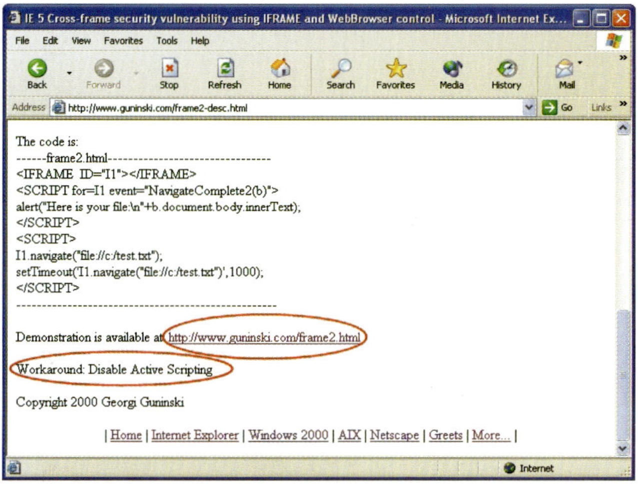

4 In addition, you also find a clear demonstration of the immediate danger.

> **Note**
>
> **Warning, danger!**
>
> The demonstrations are not always harmless. Be careful and read the notices, for it could possibly happen that your system freezes afterwards. On Guninski's Web site, you can for the most part be sure that no relevant information is deleted or spied on.

5 For the demonstration of the IFRAME problem, you must create a text file on your C drive called *Test.txt*, which you can do with a regular editor (for example, *Start/Programs/Accessories/Notepad*).

This file represents every other file that could otherwise be read. An attacker could, for example, make use of a password file always saved to the same location.

6 Even though the IFRAME option in Internet Explorer was set to *Disable* (compare page 35), the file can be read and displayed. The problem is only remedied by turning off ActiveScripting.

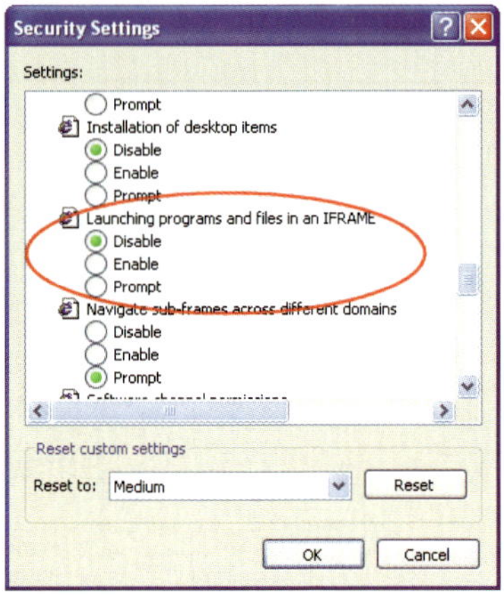

On the Web site http://www.cyscape.com/showbrow.asp, you can have your browser tested for possible weak points.

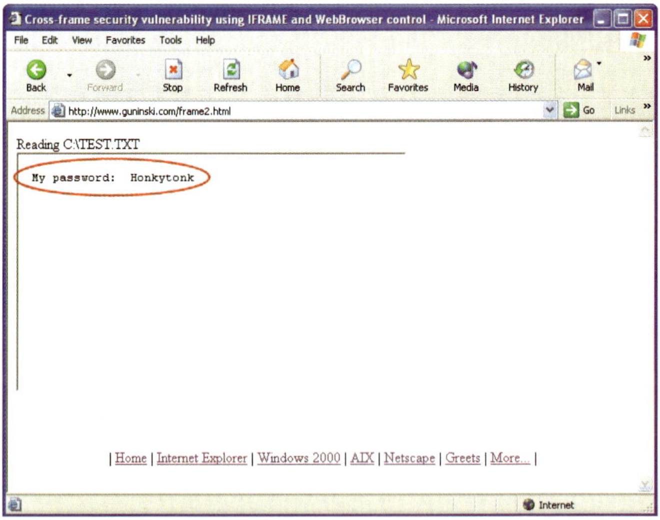

Now and then, a visit to the relevant security experts can't hurt, even if many suggestions sound like prophecies of doom and it seems that you're dealing with notorious scaremongers. Time and again, it turns out that someone is using precisely these security holes causing large amounts of damage months later. With all the recommended restrictions, though, it admittedly makes surfing less fun, for many Web developers are still of the opinion that only a Web site developed to its full potential is worthy; however, enabling all the browser's features can lead to potential danger, and you should decide for yourself what is important: short-term fun or security for your personal data and system. The Web has enough alternative sites, and, if a manufacturer believes that its Web site can't do without pizzazz, look for a more reasonable one that respects security needs and doesn't walk all over you.

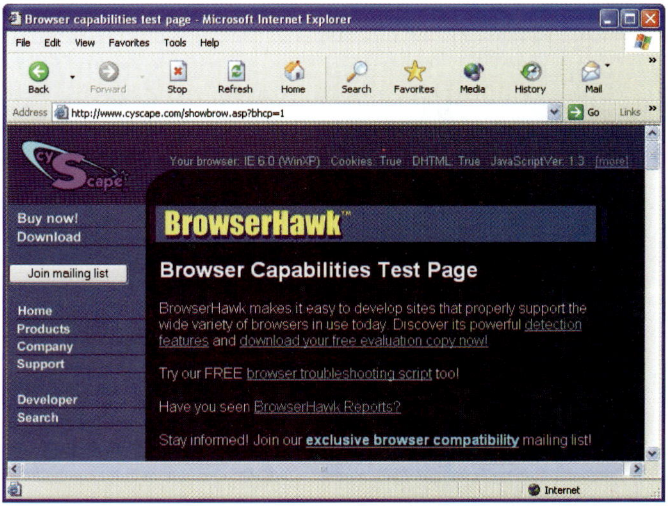

The browser's manufacturers also offer information, naturally. However, you won't find as many confessions with them about how many errors have been found, for the manufacturers don't want to scare off any customers, of course. But, in any case, you always get the most up-to-date version and also usually the error corrections (updates, bugfixes, or patches), which make a regular visit worthwhile.

Outwitting Internet Explorer updates

> **Note**
>
> **Updates from the manufacturer only**
>
> Microsoft has already made bad experiences with falsified updates that were distributed by people through e-mail and with which errors or security holes were knowingly built into the browser. Therefore, get your updates only directly from the manufacturer's Web site and never elsewhere.

2. The big picture: All of your browser security settings

Microsoft provides information about the latest security updates - that you should absolutely install if your browser requires them - on its Web site at http://www.microsoft.com/windows/ie/downloads/default.asp. Microsoft takes the middle path of assuming that buyers using its user-friendly system have no clue about how to deal with individual files. For this reason, small updates (Service Packs) that can just be exchanged for the error-ridden modules in the browser (or another application) are no longer available. Instead, you must always newly install everything, which generally means, as far as Internet Explorer is concerned, that Outlook Express and FrontPage also need to be re-installed. On the download page, you only receive a little setup program that sets up the installation after starting and gathers the installation information from the Internet afterwards. Not exactly pleasant, for you must transfer the files anew for every installation, instead of getting the data only once and then installing it on all PCs. You never know what information, other than the download, is being transferred by Microsoft (for example, the installed software?). But, luckily, you can avoid repeated downloads with a little trick, thereby reducing the danger of being spied out.:

1 Obtain the installation program for the update from the Microsoft download site (for example http://www.microsoft.com/windows/ie/downloads/ie6/default. asp) and carefully read through the notice about possible reciprocal action.

2 After downloading, use Explorer to start the program and acknowledge the agreement.

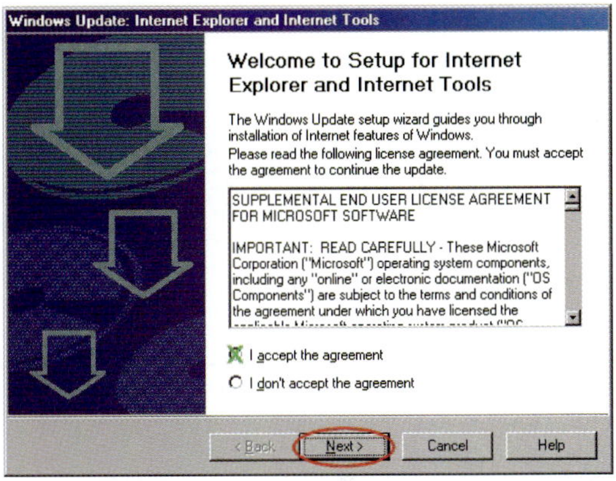

3 In the step that follows, select *Install Minimal, or customize your browser*, to force the download of the files, which you can always use again later.

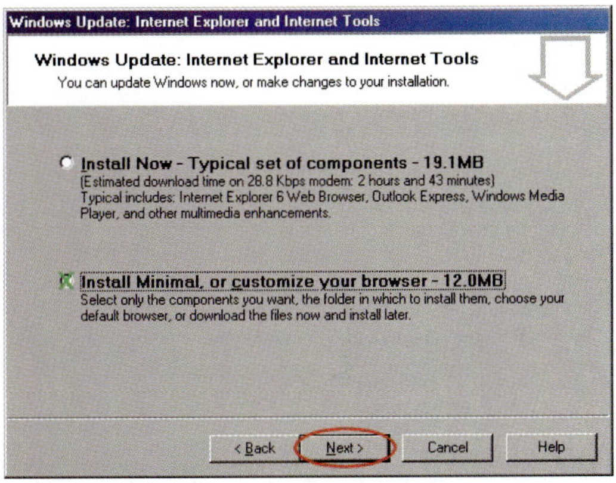

4 Click *Advanced* to go to the next step.

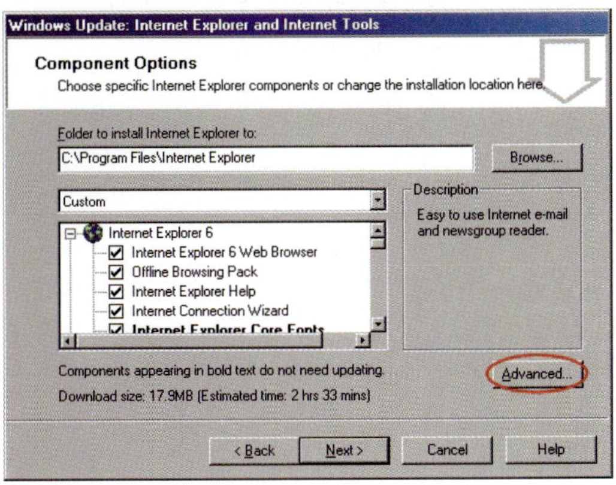

5 Enable *Download only*. This way, the files necessary for a full installation can only be fetched from the Internet once and are saved locally on your computer.

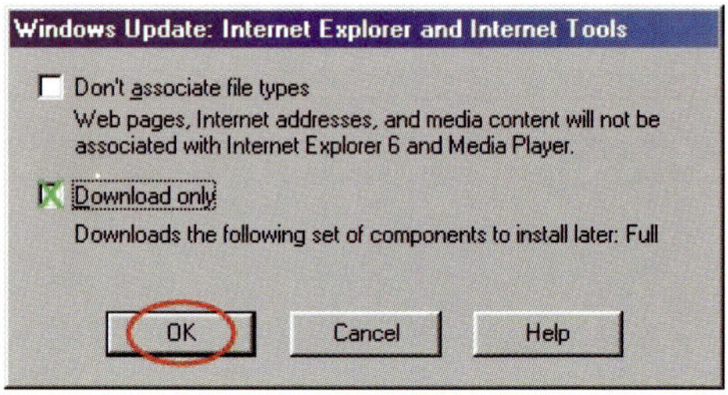

6 Back in the previous dialog window, you can see that no settings can or have to be made for the components.

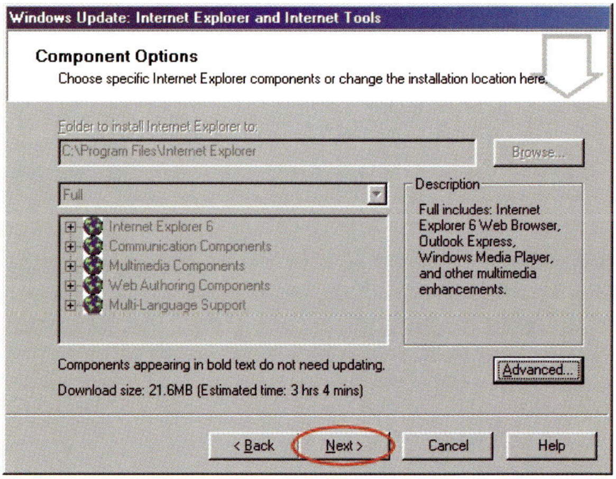

7 If necessary, click *Browse* to change the directory to which the files should be saved, and select the version of Windows for which the installation files are required. You can transfer all the necessary files for the versions you have indicated immediately. Start the file transfer by clicking *Next*, for which you can require a connection to the Internet.

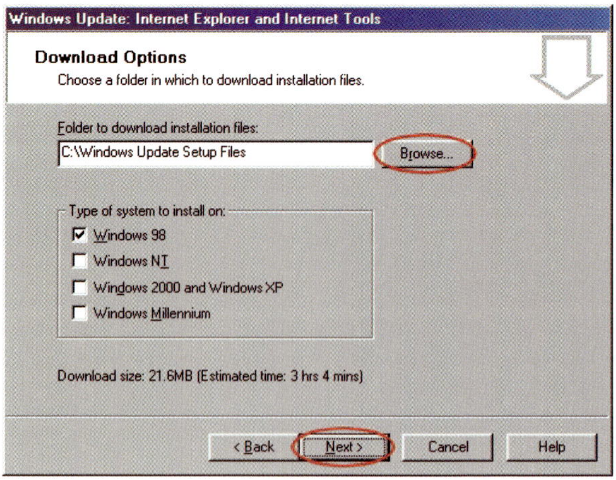

8 After the download, all the necessary files are available in the directory you previously indicated. By double-clicking the file *Ie6setup.exe*, you can start the installation program anew.

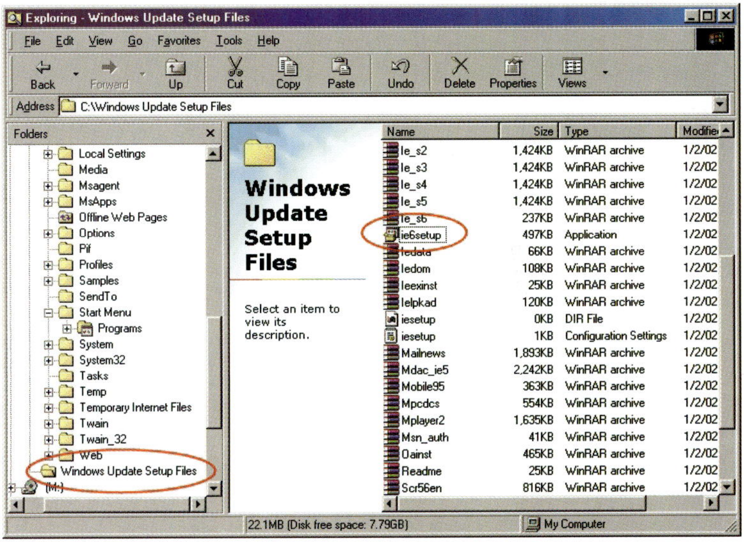

9 After accepting the license agreement, you can update the typical components with *Install Now - Typical set of components*, or manually choose the ones you want with the second option.

In any case, no more Internet connection is required by which unseen data can be transferred, and you can repeat the installation for as many computers as necessary.

3. Signed and sealed: Secure e-mails

Increasing numbers of users have come to favor e-mail as a fast, convenient, and price-worthy means of communication. Sadly, not only the number of users is increasing. Reports of e-mail bombs, chain letters, and electronically transmitted viruses are also piling up.

The most important information about e-mails and e-mailing security is provided here to prevent you from becoming a victim.

It doesn't always have to be Outlook

Microsoft sells two programs for managing e-mail (among other things): Outlook and Outlook Express. The first belongs to the Office package and must be paid for; the second comes with Internet Explorer and is free of charge. Though the detailed functions of the two programs are different, their weak points are the same.

Why Outlook is so vulnerable

1999 was a black year for all Internet users. The reports from ZDNet (http://www.zdnet.com/zdnn/stories/news/0,4586,2233116,00.html) and others should have been enough to prove to every last Internet user that the Net is a highly sensitive thing, and that even small causes can have the effect of generating millions of dollars in damage.

What had happened? A single e-mail had spread across the whole world generating increasingly more e-mails in a snowball effect. These e-mails exploded onto the Net, overloading mail systems and bringing long stretches of data traffic to a standstill (also because many large companies shut down their servers as a preventive measure).

How could a single e-mail cause so much damage? The problem was the carelessness of the users on the one hand, and the popularity and widespread use of only one e-mail program on the other. The program? MS Outlook.

The Melissa virus (which was hidden in the original e-mail as a macro) was given a single, simple task: to send an e-mail of itself to all the addresses in the recipient's address book.

Thus, once the virus arrived in an inbox, it searched the address book, generated as many copies of itself as there were entries, and sent these copies to many more inboxes, where it repeated the same action. Often enough, the virus hit upon company directories, which put thousands of employee and customer addresses at its disposal.

Melissa's sole weakness: its whole scheme only worked if the recipient used Outlook. The address books of other e-mail programs could not be used in the same manner, and the virus faced a dead end.

Whenever a malicious hacker wants to carry out an attack through e-mail, he can rely on the fact that Outlook is one of the most widespread programs. Once he finds a security hole, he can exploit it without mercy and bring damage to millions of users, without having to even think about other programs.

And thus it happened a year later: the I Love You virus spread like wildfire, as if the Internet community hadn't learned a thing.

Free alternatives

Because Outlook is vulnerable as an e-mail program, it is only natural to think about alternatives. Other programs may offer not only more protection but also features not available in Outlook. Although Outlook needs a comparatively large amount of hard drive space and has a costly professional version, free alternatives abound.

For Windows users, Qualcomm (http://www.qualcomm.com) offers a popular program that emulates Outlook in its outer appearance and control structure. Eudora is a capable e-mail client that leaves nothing to be desired.

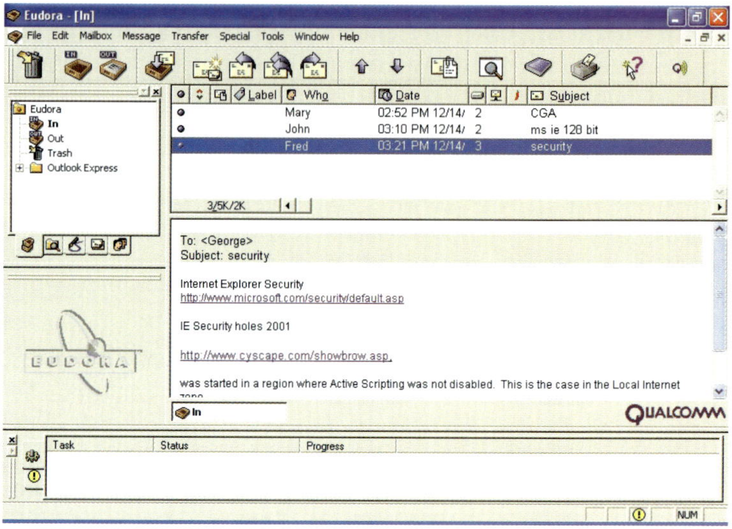

You can download the current version (5.1) of the 6 MB program from Eudora's home page at www.eudora.com. After the installation, you can decide which version of Eudora you want to use:

- the Light mode, which has fewer functions but is free of charge
- the Sponsored mode, which is financed through ads
- the Pay mode, in which you get the full power of Eudora without ads

Select the mode for which you want to import the data, and Eudora does the rest.

If you have worked with another e-mail program like Outlook or Netscape, you'll be able to switch without a problem.

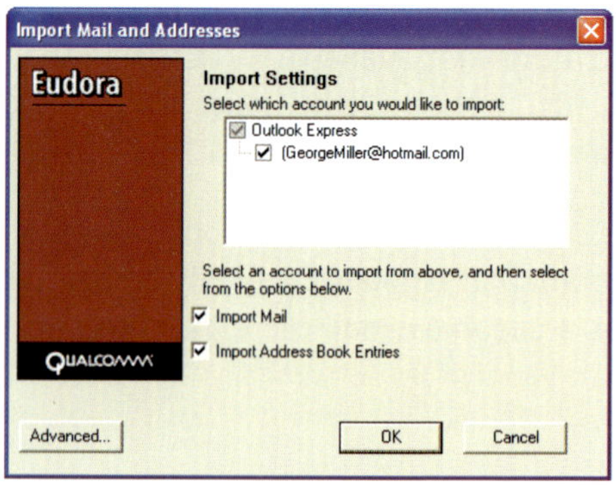

Eudora offers to import your previous settings, e-mail, and addresses over the *File/Import* menu.

Note

Free Web based e-mail

Providers like MSN (http://www.msn.com) and Yahoo (http://www.yahoo.com/) offer you a special service: an e-mail address of your own, chosen by you, for free and for life. You can then regulate your entire correspondence over the Web site of the provider. Good providers even offer you the alternative of working with an e-mail program offline.

Handling e-mails correctly

No matter which e-mail program you use, if you use it incorrectly, your e-mails can be used to sabotage your system. Keep your eyes open and use your common sense every time you send or receive an e-mail message. This is how you can e-mail securely:

Don't format in HTML

You have been paying attention to everything in your browser, but a Trojan still managed to smuggle itself into your system. For instance, you have just received an HTML e-mail that contained an executable program code embedded in the HTML code, and your e-mail client did nothing to prevent it.

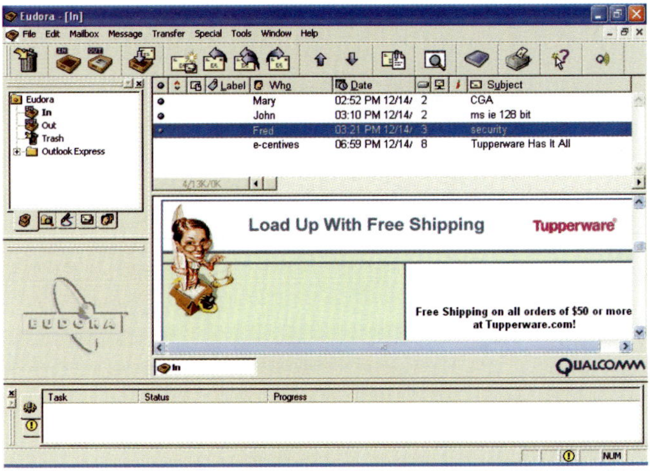

3. Signed and sealed: Secure e-mails

E-mails have been around for a long time, and in the past they were made up only of simple characters. No one even dreamed of formatting e-mails with colors, images, character settings, and so forth. As e-mail grew more and more popular, this changed, and ways were sought to make formatting possible. It's a relatively simple trick: the editor offers all the usual formatting possibilities known from text editing and generates an HTML page before sending the e-mail. There's only one catch:

HTML takes up appreciably more space than plain text.

- Because many users don't want to or cannot display HTML formatting, both forms (the formatted and the unformatted text) are often sent in the same e-mail, increasing the size of the e-mail even more.
- The HTML code can hide the previously mentioned commands that are targeting your system.
- In addition, such commands can create a connection to the Internet and transfer further data from the page of the sender. The sender of the Trojan cannot only find out that you have read the e-mail but can spy on you regularly.

This e-mail from spree.com accesses the server to load missing images.

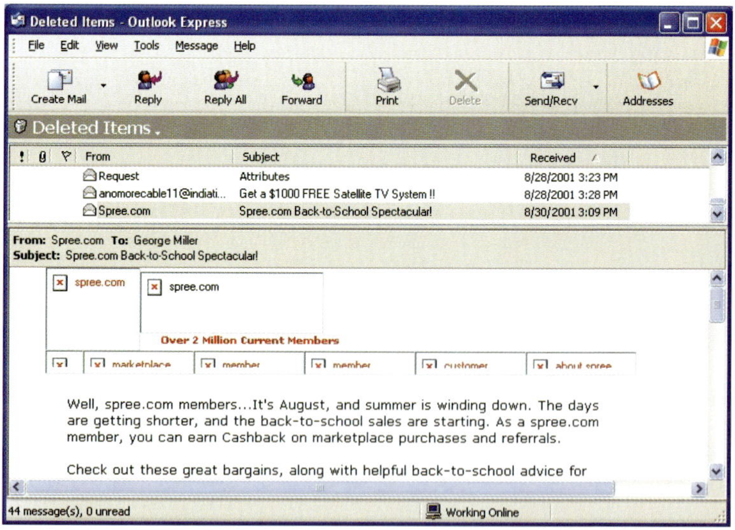

A look at the HTML code of many e-mails (for instance from spree.com) reveals that among the many images that are to be loaded from the server, there is an imaginary picture. Loading this "image" actually transmits data that looks suspiciously like the one in the header of the message. The sender thus learns not only that the e-mail has reached its destination (that is, that the address exists and he can keep spamming it), but also that you have read the message – a modern form of confirmation of receipt, if you will.

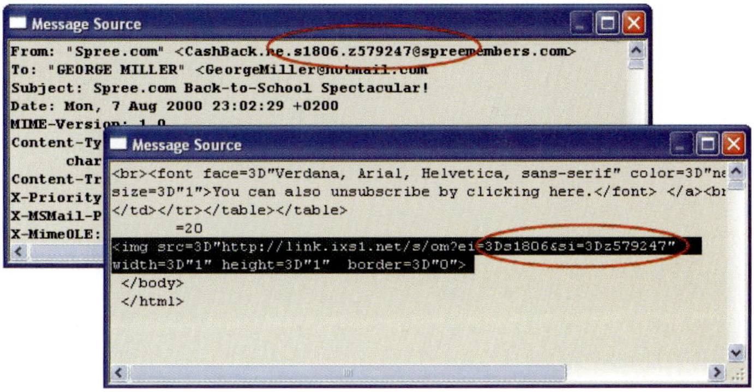

> **If you don't want to sacrifice the formatting**
>
> In this case, you can attach a file (for example, as PDF, see page 68) containing the formatted text to your e-mail. The recipient then has the possibility of deciding what to do with the file and can thus be protect better.

You should sacrifice the formatting entirely, in order not to annoy your correspondent.

The well-known e-mail programs Outlook (Express) and Eudora are unfortunately unable to hide HTML e-mails. If you receive an e-mail formatted in HTML, it is displayed. You can still obtain a small degree of security, however, and make life more difficult for dyed-in-the-wool spammers:

3. Signed and sealed: Secure e-mails

1 In Outlook (Express), go to the *Tools/Options* menu and switch to the *Security* tab. Enable the option *Restricted site zone*. You can adjust the security settings for this zone as described in the chapter about security settings for the browsers, starting with page 28.

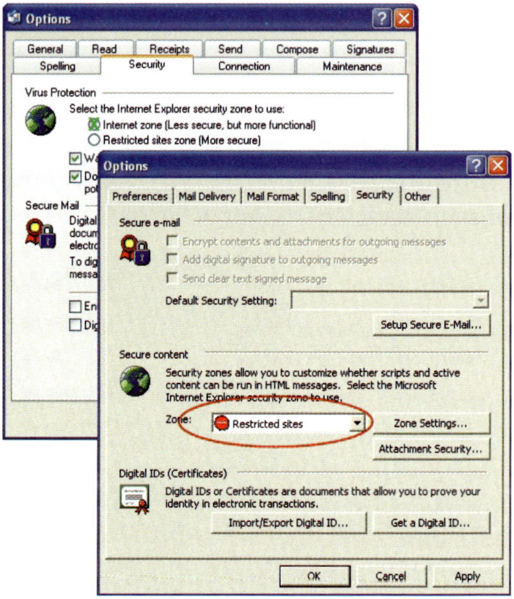

2 In Eudora, call up the *Options* dialog window by going to *Tools/Options*. Switch to the *Viewing Mail* category and deactivate *Use Microsoft's viewer* and *Allow executables in HTML content*. Unlike the internal mail display in the Microsoft program, the one in Eudora displays fewer HTML formats; it only displays executable HTML content that is critical.

Hidden information in the header can be viewed by anybody

In the header of each e-mail a simple function is hidden that allows you as the recipient to access a whole host of information. The header registers where the message is coming from, over which computers it was routed and who else received a copy.

This way, you can learn a lot about the sender, and you might even get to e-mail addresses that are none of your business, because they are those of the sender's private correspondents. The reverse can also happen, of course: you, too, divulge your contacts through your e-mails.

All e-mail programs are usually set to hide the majority of the information in the header and to show it only when prompted.

- In Outlook Express, you can view the additional information for the currently selected e-mail on the *Details* tab of the *File/Properties* menu, not by going to *View/All Headers* as you would expect. However, Outlook Express doesn't display all the information contained in the header.

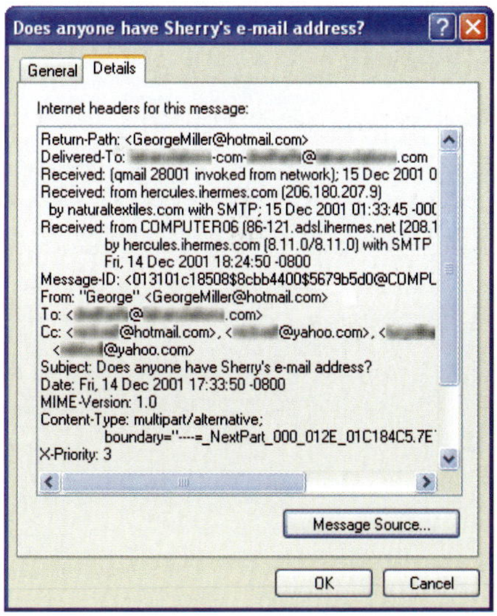

- In Outlook, you must open the message in a separate window by double-clicking it. You can then view the entire content of the e-mail header under *View/Options*.

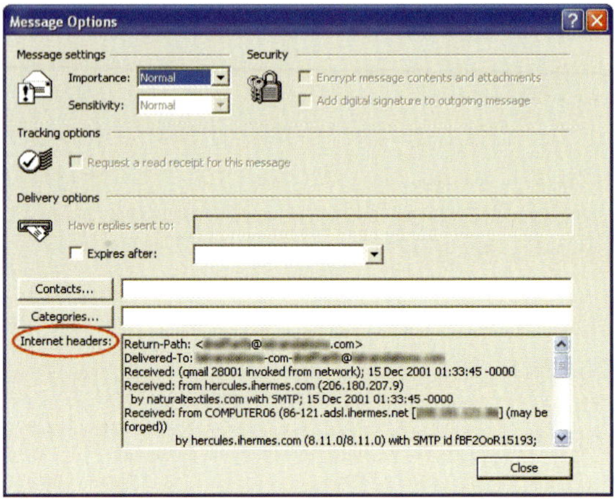

- In Eudora, you must also open the e-mail in a separate window by double-clicking it. Then, click the aptly named *Blah Blah Blah* button to view all header entries.

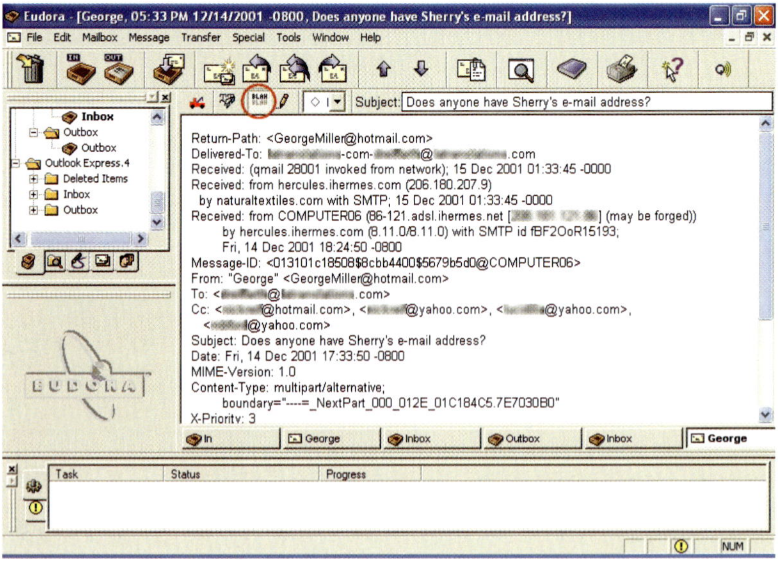

E-mail headers are revealing. The most important header entries contain the following information:

Header	Meaning
Return-Path	This is the e-mail address that is entered into the To field when the recipient answers. It usually corresponds to the sender's address, but the sender can enter a different address here.
Delivered-To	The message was delivered successfully.
Received	This information should be read from the bottom up. Every e-mail client who receives and relays the message adds a line with its information. This way, you know exactly over which computers the message was routed and when it was received there.
Message-ID	When a message is sent, it receives an ID under which it can be cataloged by the mail server of the sender. With this information, one can complain about a message to the provider of the mail server, who can then identify the sender.
From	The sender (the e-mail address from which the message was sent). It is illegal to fake this information.
To	All recipients including the address of the message.
Subject	The subject of the message.
Date	Date and time according to the sender's data (the system time).
Content-Type	The format of the message. T*ext/plain* means that the message is plain text; *text/html* that it was formatted in HTML.
X-Mailer	Name of the e-mail program used.

With a little effort, one can find out a lot about the sender - which could be used for an immediate attack - as well as about other users. Most of these values cannot be (legally) manipulated, fortunately or unfortunately. You can't do anything for your privacy, that's true, but you can at least trust that other senders' information is correct.

The time saved with the *Date* has no weight of proof, for instance, because it gives the system time of the computer on which the e-mail was written, which can be easily manipulated. You can rely on the information under *Received*, however, to tell you when the message was really sent, because the mail servers usually set the correct time automatically. The offsets after the time show the discrepancy between the local time and GMT (**G**reenwich **M**ean **T**ime). In the example above, you can tell that the first server received the e-mail only a little while after it was sent out (EST = **E**astern **S**tandard **T**ime, where it is five hours earlier than GMT: *-0005*). Only seconds later, the e-mail was received by the second server, which was in GMT time, with an offset of *-0000*.

With the knowledge of the X-Mailer of the sender, one can direct a hacker attack precisely against the user. Because the hacker knows which system he encounters, he can deliberately use the system's weaknesses.

The information under *To* is entirely at the sender's disposal, and it is a sign of terrible foolishness if a list of all recipients is displayed here. As a recipient, I can thus find out who else has received a copy; not to mention that a number of new e-mail addresses are in this way played right into my hands. If I am a spammer, I will surely rub my hands in anticipation of spamming all these new users.

Only when all recipients know each other and want to communicate among themselves, should the recipients' information be displayed under *To*.

If you don't want to commit this faux pas and give away your friends, acquaintances, and so forth, don't use the *To* or *Cc* (**c**arbon **c**opy) fields, in which you then divide all recipients' addresses with commas. Instead, you should enter one recipient under *To* and use *Bcc* (**b**lind **c**arbon **c**opy) for the rest (the addresses should be divided by commas here as well).

The mail server sends a copy of the e-mail to all addresses entered under *Bcc*, but replaces the *To* information with the address of each recipient without transmitting the content of the *Bcc* field. This way, the recipients can't see who else has received the e-mail.

Note

Using Outlook (Express) correctly

Microsoft hides the *Bcc* field in its e-mail clients by default. In Outlook, you can unhide the field for a new e-mail by going to *Options/Bcc*; in Outlook Express by going to *View/All Headers*.

Bcc is used correctly here.

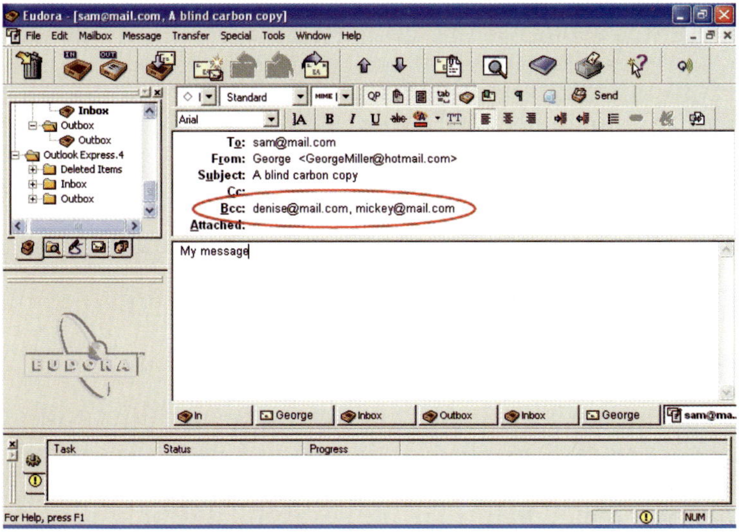

Don't trust any e-mail attachments

The worst e-mail viruses (or worms) of the past weren't located in the e-mail per se but in an attached file. Depending on the file type, they had and have different effects.

- If the virus is an executable program (usually recognizable by the ending *.exe*), the program can do anything it wants. A single command is then enough to format your hard drive and delete all your data within seconds.
- Visual Basic macros can be recognized by the ending *.vbs*. They, too, are basically programs with the same possibilities.
- Sending Word or other MS Office files is also very popular, for they, too, can contain destructive macros. In the First Aid section, you can find an example (page 16), of how simple the design of such a macro is and how you can test your acquaintances.

> **Note**
>
> **Always save first**
>
> Generally, you should never open an attachment directly out of the e-mail program. You should instead save the attachment to the hard drive first and scan it for viruses. This is especially important for attachments you weren't expecting and whose senders you don't know. But beware: Even attachments from known senders can be dangerous. After all, such well-known viruses like Melissa send themselves to addresses out of personal address directories; thus, they can come from people you know.

1 First, save the attachment to your hard drive. This way, you can use your virus scanner to check the file.

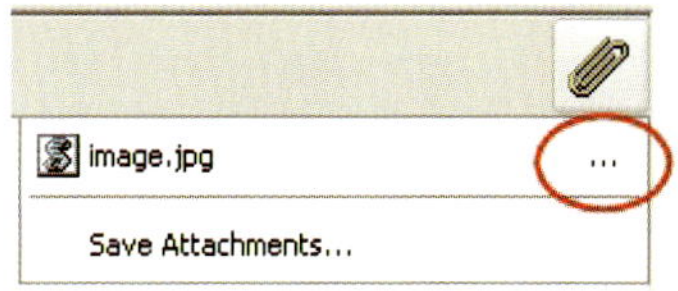

2 Start Explorer and take a close look at the file. If you are using Windows XP, the security hole we are about to explain has been somewhat plugged, because a description of the suspicious file is given by default:

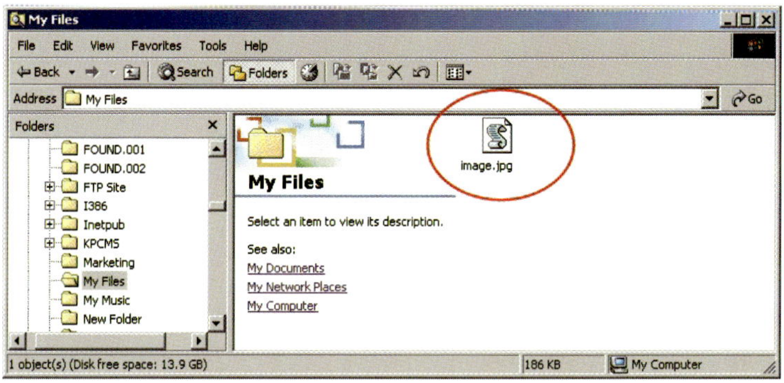

If you are using an older version of Windows, read on. In the example, the file (*image.jpg. .vbs*) exploits two weaknesses in Windows:

- The file name is very long. Spaces have been inserted between the first part of the name and the file extension. As a consequence, only the beginning of the file name is displayed (which was chosen in such a way as to suggest that the file is an image and not a VBS program). The small dots suggest hidden information, but they are easy to overlook (starting with the display in Outlook).

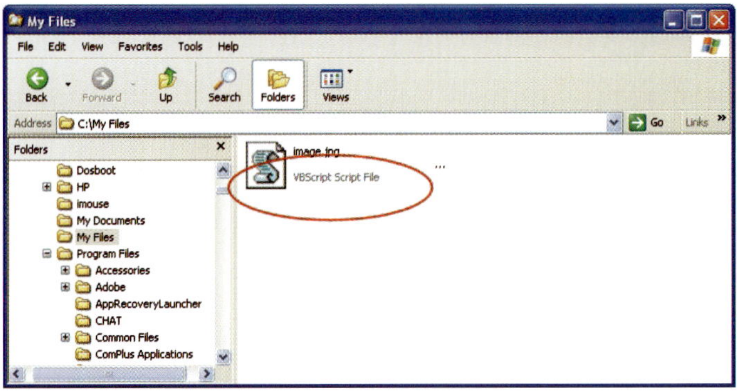

- In its default setting, Explorer doesn't even display the tell-tale extension.

For increased security, you can optimize Explorer's settings. Go to *View/Folder Options* and switch to the *View* tab. Disable the option *Hide file extensions for known file types*. The suffix *.vbs* is now displayed, and you have exposed the culprit.

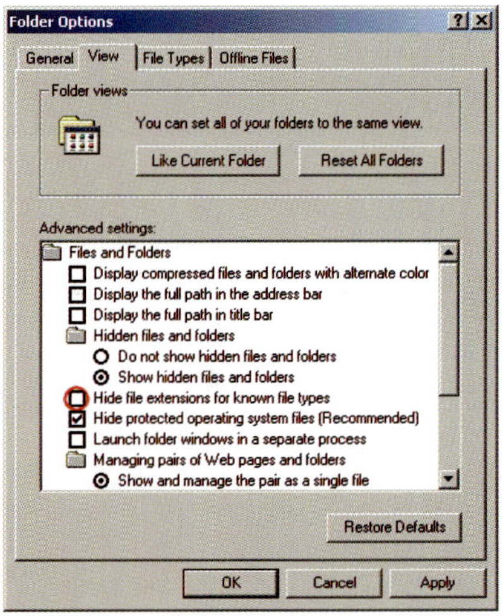

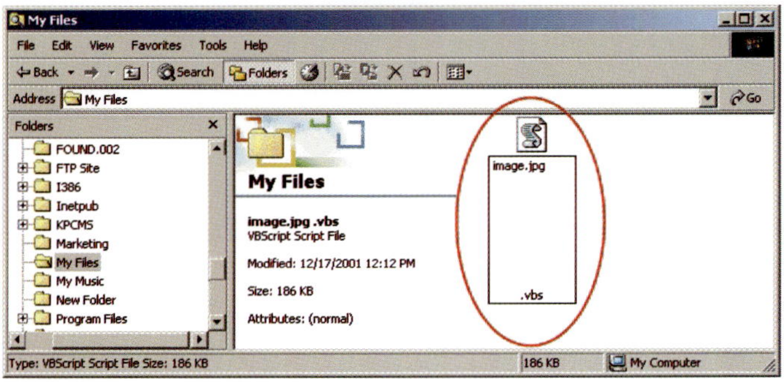

Document formats you can trust

Until recently, you could blindly trust many file formats because they couldn't hide any viruses or harm anything. Win2K.Streams was the first virus that could afflict any file. However, this virus exploits a peculiarity of the **NT** **F**ile **S**ystem (NTFS), which means that you don't have to worry about other file systems (for example, Windows 9x or ME, which use the FAT file system).

Apart from that, there are files, however, that are potentially at risk, as well as others that are entirely harmless. The most secure include all the picture formats, like GIF, JPG, BMP, and so on, and ASCII text files (*.txt*).

When sending e-mails, you can't always know what system the recipient uses. For this reason, it's not recommended to use file types that cannot be guaranteed to be viewed by everyone. For instance, it is impolite to attach text files written in Word for Windows, because users of other programs cannot read these (or only with effort), and might even be reluctant to open them knowing about the macro viruses and other problems they may hide.

The **R**ich **T**ext **F**ormat (*.rtf*) is a considerably better choice for file sharing, for this format can be created and opened in any text editor without risks. As a universal format, it is also widely used.

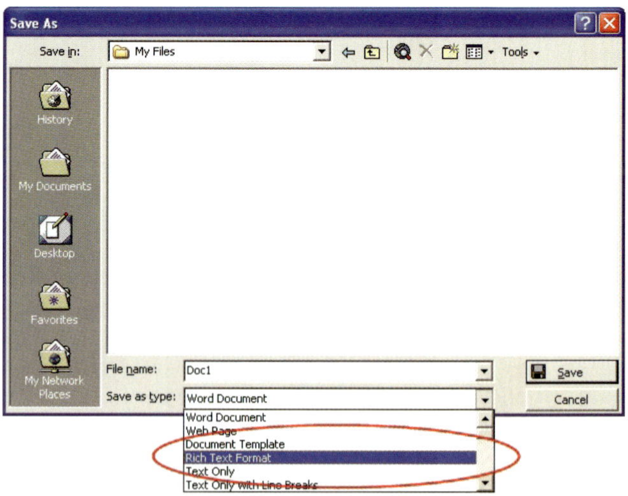

RTF does harbor a risk in connection with Word for Windows, however, for it is easy to rename a DOC file containing macro viruses to a "harmless" RTF file. When you double-click the file and Word starts up, it treats the file like a normal Microsoft Word document, as you can find out for yourself:

1 Create the macro described in the immediate measures on page 16 and save the Word file as described (for example, as *macro.doc*).

2 Start Windows Explorer and change the suffix of the Word document from *.doc* to *.rtf* by going to *File/Rename*. To do so, you first must change the folder options for Explorer as described on page 67.

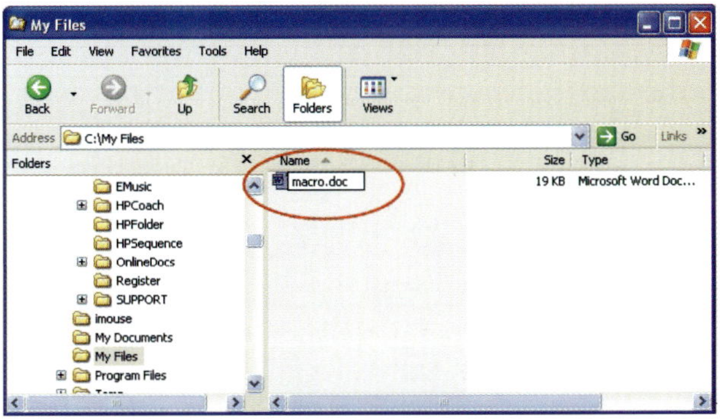

3 Acknowledge the confirmation prompt in Windows by clicking *Yes*, because a file never becomes unusable if it's renamed.

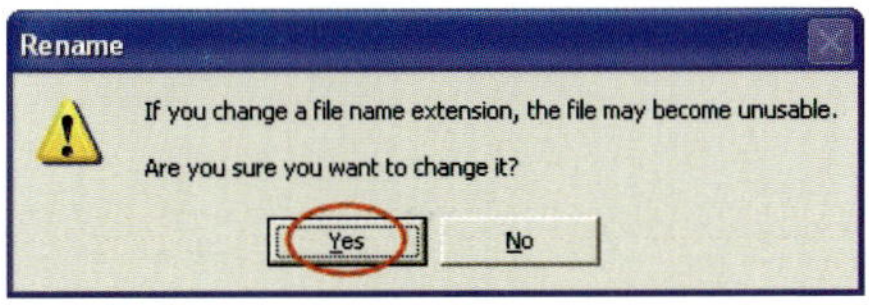

4 Now, double-click the file name and open the RTF file in Word. Although the file was assumed to be safe, the macro is executed, and the unsuspecting user who went by the suffix *.rtf* can incur damage.

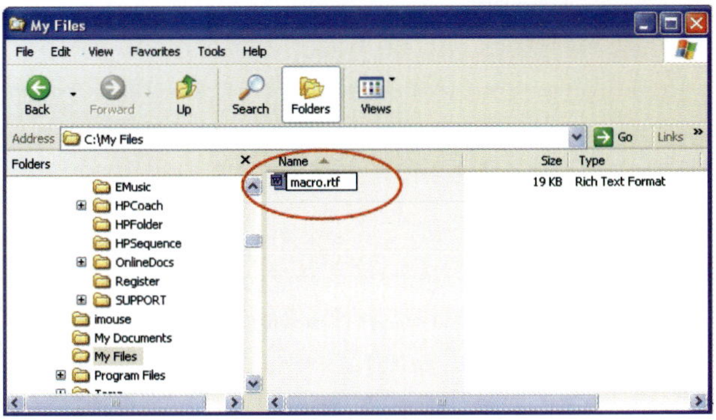

Another format for sharing data on the Internet is PDF, introduced by Adobe (http://www.acrobat.com). You can generate a PDF document with the Acrobat Distiller. The pages can then be viewed with Acrobat Reader (see illustration), which is available for free for any system. PDF is extremely practical because it cannot spread viruses or macros. In addition, the program for viewing the files is free and compatible with every operating system. The files can contain any formatting of the original text editor. The only shortcoming is that the Distiller (which you need to create PDF files) is not free and therefore not yet widespread

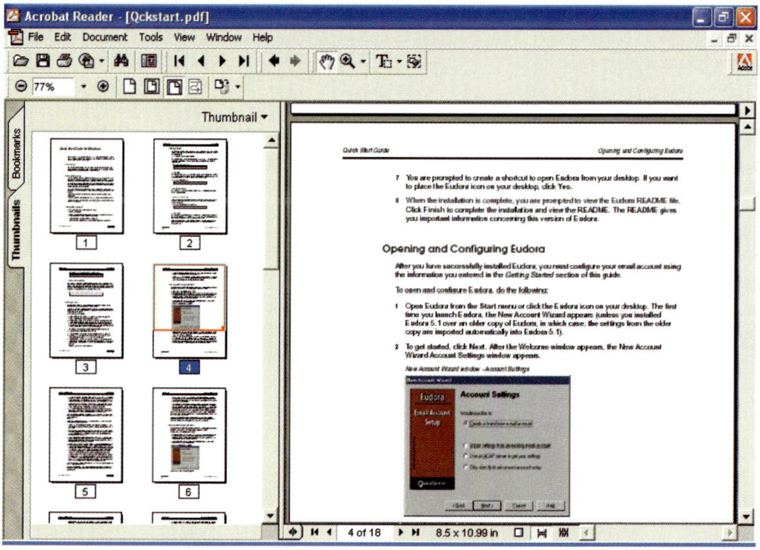

Have you ever been upset about the fact that e-mails give the name of the sender so that messages can be traced back to the person who sent them? Giving away your identity while e-mailing isn't necessary, however, for you can send messages anonymously using remailers. If you want to order a catalog, for example, or participate in a contest without being spammed to death, you may want to consider a remailer.

Your e-mail is then sent to a special computer that receives the message, removes all tell-tale information and relays it to the intended destination. You can even send the message through a chain of remailers, so that your e-mail hits a number of intermediate stops before being delivered at its destination, which does even a better job of removing all traces.

Note

Remailers are a serious thing

Remailers are a great thing, but they are intended for sending e-mails anonymously to protect the sender from any sort of reprisals. They are not intended for getting away with spreading threats, harassments, or unwanted advertising. If a remailer administrator should find out about any such mischief, he can use the logs to identify the malefactor.

Numerous Help programs, like the classic Private Idahoe, assist you with using remailers. However, you can also write a normal e-mail and send it to a remailer. To influence how the e-mail is relayed, you only need to enter a few extra indications in the text area:

1 Go to http://anon.efga.org/Remailers/TypeIList for a list of type-I remailers (the kind of remailers you want to use). At the beginning of the page, you can find the functions and addresses (in angle brackets) of the providers (the explanations are at the bottom of the page). The second table shows you how long it takes for a message to be relayed.

2 In your e-mail program, create the message you want to render anonymous. Enter one of the remailers as the destination.

3 It doesn't matter what *Subject* you enter, for the remailer removes it.

4 For the remailer to know what to do with your e-mail, you need to incorporate some commands in the text area. They must bes written as shown in the following.

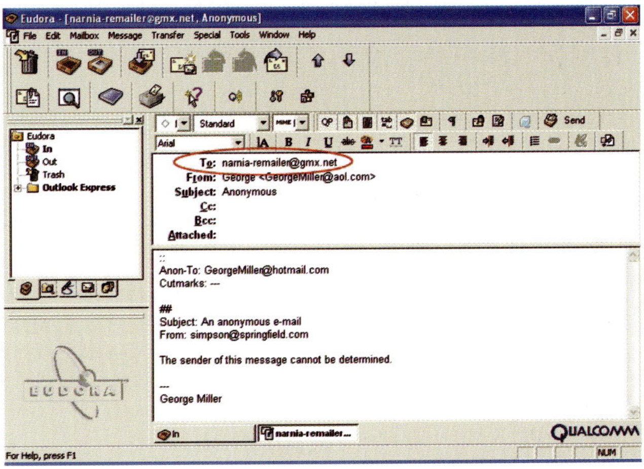

5 First, enter two colons, followed by "Anon-To:" and the e-mail address of the real recipient.

6 If you want to cut out some text (for instance, to leave out the signature which might give you away), enter the characters starting with which you want to cut the text after "Cutmarks:"

> **Note**
>
> **Signatures give you away**
>
> If you use a signature that is automatically appended to every e-mail, and the signature contains such information as your home page, for instance, you may lose your anonymity. Cut the signature off by using cutmarks, or remove the information in the editor.

7 Enter a double hash character, followed by "Subject:" and the subject that should be visible to the recipient.

8 Some remailers support further information, like entering a fictional sender after "From:"

9 In the end, enter the actual text of your e-mail and send the message as usual. Depending on the speed of the remailer, your recipient soon gets mail. Some remailers send you confirmation that the message was relayed.

> **Note**
>
> **Test the remail service on yourself**
>
> For a quick taste of remailing, you can send a message by a remailer to yourself. Simply enter your own address after "Anon-To:"

The illustration shows an anonymized e-mail that provides no clues as to the sender. The subject and the sender were changed. All additional tell-tale information was removed from the header.

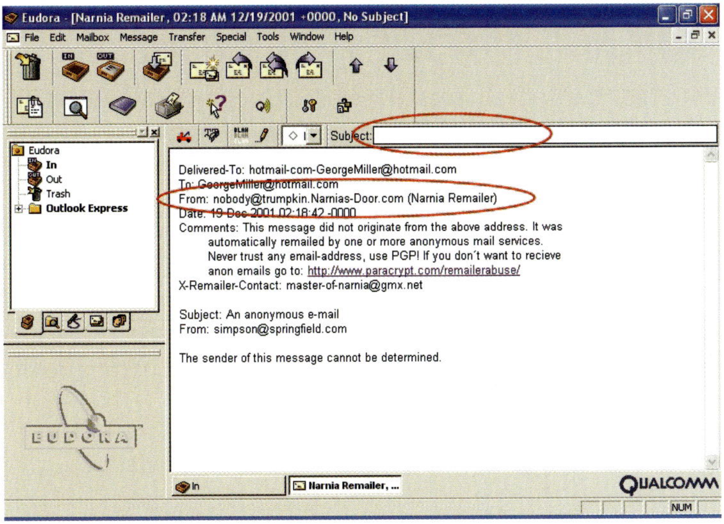

If entering the additional commands is too much effort for you, you can also use one of the many Web front ends like the one from Riot Anonymous Remailer (https://riot.eu.org/cgi/remailer.cgi) or http://www.no-id.com/remail.cgi, where you can type your e-mail directly and choose the remailers with which you want to anonymize it.

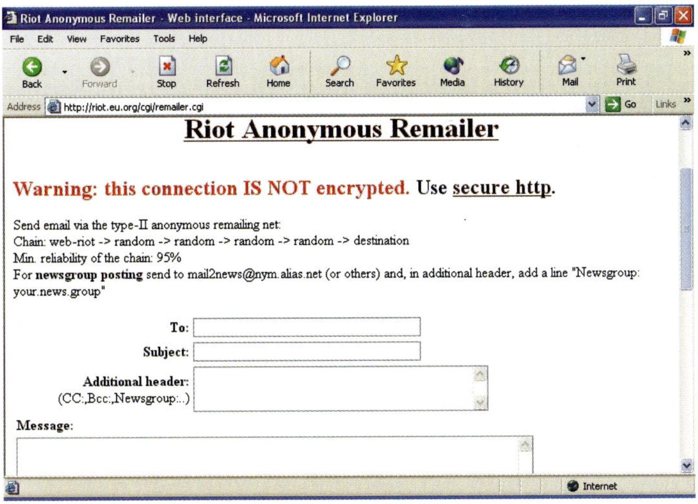

https://riot.eu.org/cgi/remailer.cgi

Sign and encrypt your e-mail

With the many advantages of e-mails comes a big disadvantage: how can you ever know that the e-mail really comes from the given sender and that the content wasn't manipulated or even read by a third party?

You can think of your e-mail as a postcard: anybody can enter any sender information he/she chooses, and the card can be read by any number of people while underway, for it passes through many hands. Someone could even change the content. The same is true of e-mails, for the message transfers through many systems, and you may have the bad luck of it encountering someone along the way who decides to do more than relay your message.

In everyday life, you probably use a sealed letter when you want to protect important information from prying eyes. An electronic message cannot be inserted into an envelope, but the content can be encrypted and safe-guarded against forgery with a digital signature.

How does it work?

The standard for secure e-mail traffic is pretty much set by the freeware Pretty Good Privacy (PGP). In addition to other functions, PGP offers two all-important features:

- Any text can be encrypted in such a way as to render the original text unreadable. Only authorized persons can decipher the text then. The process is so secure as to be prohibited in several countries. Until a few years ago, it even fell under the US weapon export embargo, for even the most powerful mainframe computers have difficulty cracking the code.
- A message (whether encrypted or not) can be signed with a digital signature. This ensures that the text cannot be changed at a later time and that the sender information isn't forged.

For private correspondence, encrypting messages may rarely be necessary, but it might often prove important to use signatures to verify the authenticity of the sender (for example, for bank transactions, orders, advertisements, cancellations, and so forth) if you want to show the recipient that you are trustworthy.

PGP uses public key cryptography with asymmetric encryption. This sounds impressive but is a rather simple process:

1 The program creates a pair of keys for you: a public one (yellow) and a private one (blue).

2 You protect the private key with a password and guard it like the apple of your eye. Never give it away. Imagine what would happen if you lost the key and someone who could also guess your password found it

3 As the name implies, the public key is meant for the public. You need to give a copy of the public key to anyone who wants to send you an encrypted message or who wants to verify your digital signature. To ensure better access to your key - for the more people have it, the better - leave it on a key server (something like a public key rack).

The two keys can be used to encrypt e-mails:

1 To encrypt a message or file, the sender uses your public key and then sends you the coded message.

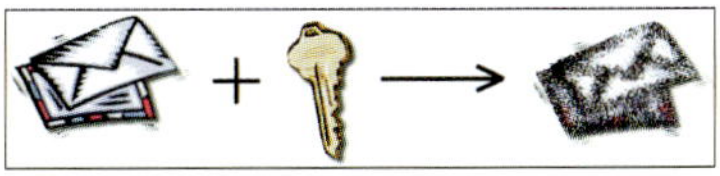

2 When you get the message, you can decode it with the private key.

If you want to send a message and proof your authenticity to the recipient, sign the text with your private key. In principle, it's worth signing every message you send. Even if the recipient doesn't (yet) use PGP, she can see that you are using it and that you are interested in secure communication. If nothing else, your gesture creates trust (for instance with a potential employer), and if the recipient is interested, she can install PGP and verify your signature.

1 If you want to send a message and prove your authenticity to the recipient, sign the text with your private key. You can also encrypt the message. To do so, you need the public key of the recipient, however.

2 The recipient can then use your public key to establish that you are really the one who composed the message, and that the message hasn't been manipulated underway.

Casting S/MIME aside

The e-mail clients of both Outlook (Express) and Netscape support the asymmetric encryption process S/MIME, which, like PGP, was also conceived to send encrypted messages and ensure secure e-mailing. To send or receive encrypted messages, you first must get a certificate that identifies you with the recipient as the legitimate sender.

You can obtain such a certificate from VeriSign (http://www.verisign.com), for instance. You can then test it free of charge for 60 days, after which you must pay a yearly fee of $15. Because of this charge, S/MIME has so far had little success in the private sector, for PGP offers more features free of charge, and its user environment leaves nothing to be desired as well.

How to install PGP

Note

Do you have the current version?

If you want to run PGP under Windows ME, you need a current program version, for the system finds fault with any version under 6.5.3. Currently no version is available specifically for Windows XP; however, PGP for Windows 2000 should do the job.

For the most current version for your system, go to the *Download* section of the International PGP Home Page at http://www.pgpi.org. After downloading the roughly 8 MB program, you need to install it, for which you need an unzip program like WinZip (http://www.winzip.com), unless you are using Windows XP:

1 To open the PGP archive, double-click the file name in Explorer. In Windows XP, you are brought to a zipped folder screen; otherwise, WinZip is launched.

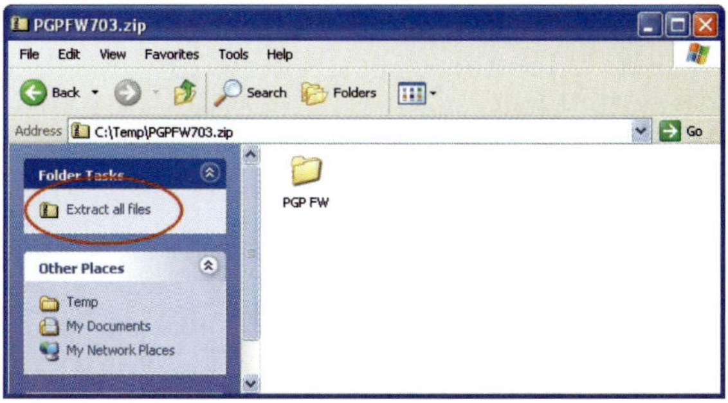

2 In Windows XP, click *Extract all files*. A Wizard guides you through the extraction process. In Winzip, select *Actions/Extract*. In the dialog window that follows, select the directory to which you want to unzip the archive. Enable the option *All files* to unzip all files and click *Extract*.

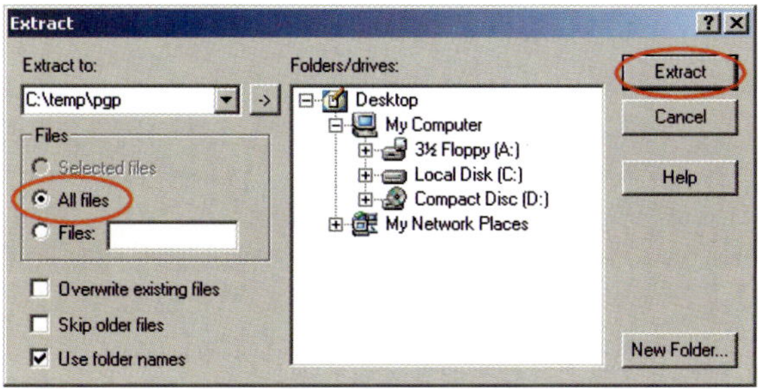

3 Once the extraction has been completed, you can continue. Double-click the installation file *PGPfreewareX.X.X.exe* (where *X* is the version number) to start it. First, make sure that no e-mail program is running, however. Otherwise, the installer brings it to your attention.

4 If an older version of PGP is already installed on your computer, the installation program notifies you of this and might automatically uninstall it. Acknowledge the welcome screen by clicking *Next*.

5 Read the licensing agreement and confirm it with *Yes*.

6 You can also skip the information about all the innovations by clicking *Next*.

7 On the screen that follows, you are asked if you already possess any key rings. If you have used PGP in the past, reply with *Yes*. Setup then queries the two files *Pubring.skr* and *Secring.skr*. You only need to click the appropriate file, and the program imports the older keys.

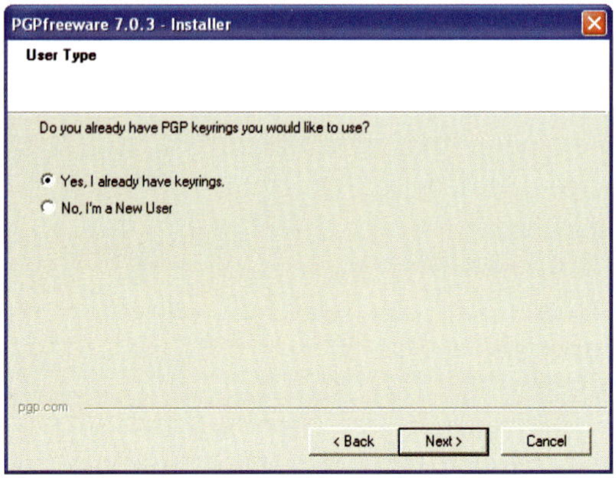

8 If you want to, you can select a different installation directory by clicking *Browse*, or you can confirm the one being shown by clicking *Next*.

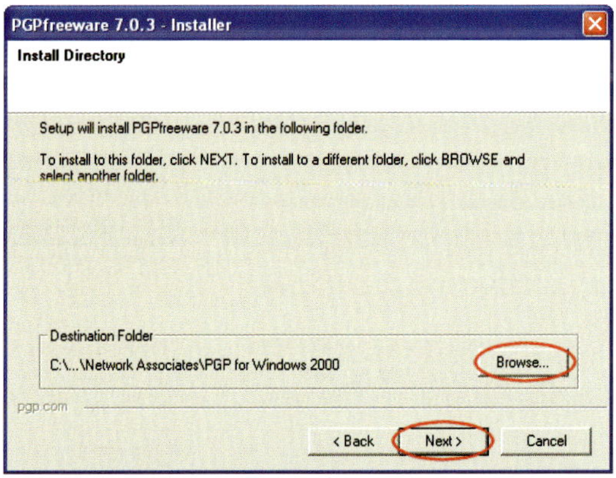

9 In the dialog box that follows, select the components you want to install. If you want to, you can disable PGPnet. PGPnet allows you to exchange encrypted data over the Internet with a partner. Also, if you are installing the Windows 2000 version of PGP in a Windows XP operating system, enabling PGPnet might have adverse effects on your system. Besides, this fea-

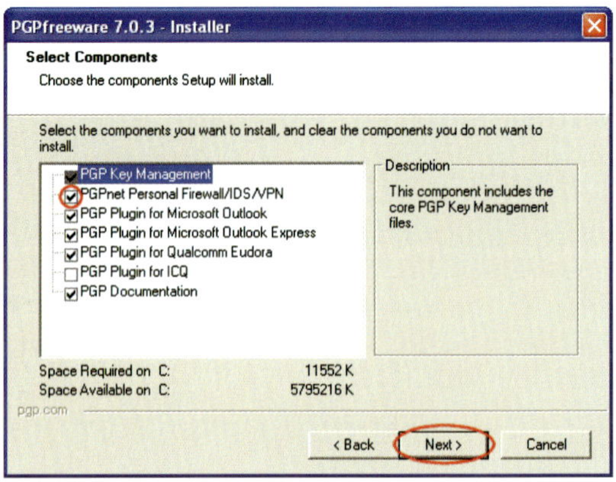

ture won't increase your security while surfing the Web, and if you need it, you can always install it later. Leave all plug-in options enabled, so all your e-mail programs can be optimized.

10 Before starting the installation, verify the settings by clicking *Next*.

11 Click *Finish* to restart your PC.

The one thing you are still missing at this point is a key pair with a private and a public key. PGP helps you create the pair, of course, and you can encrypt your first e-mail within minutes.

1 Start PGPkeys by going to *Start/Programs/PGP*. You can also start it by right-clicking the new PGP icon in the tray bar and selecting *PGPkeys*. If you have imported already existing keys during setup, they are now displayed.

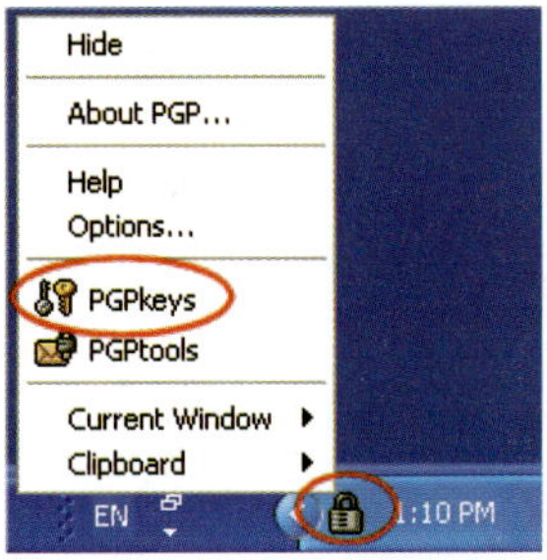

2 To create a new key pair, start the Wizard by going to *Keys/New Key*. The first dialog window shortly explains to you the meanings of the public and private keys. Clicking *Next* generates a key using the most common options. Click *Expert* to personally select the key's characteristics:

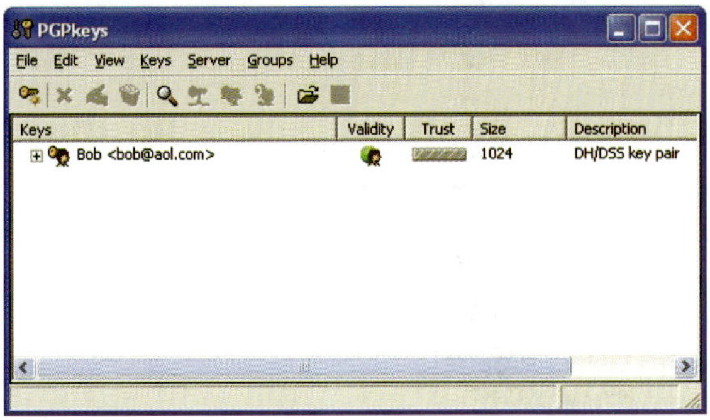

3 To create a new key pair, start the Wizard by going to *Keys/New Key*. The first dialog window explains to you the meanings of the public and private keys. You can skip this explanation by clicking *Next*.

4 Now enter your *Full name* (first and last) and your correct *Email address*..

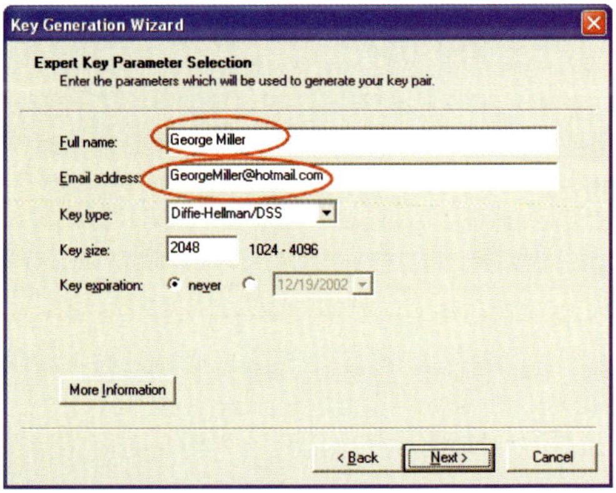

5 PGP supports two different types of keys. For new keys, you should use *Diffie-Hellman/DSS* instead of the older *RSA* system, because they are more secure. (If you don't choose the *Expert* option, this is the default).

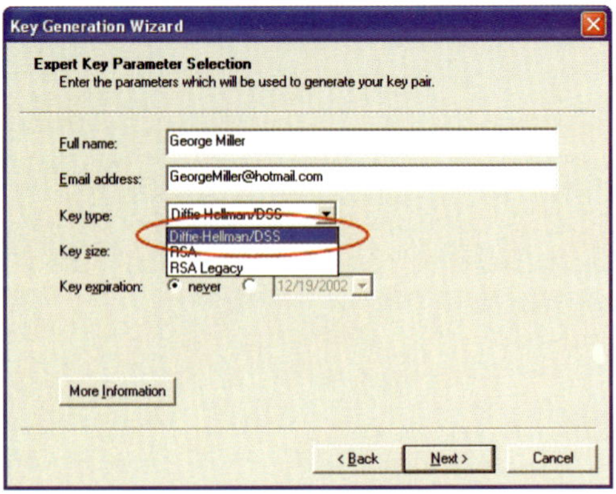

6 The longer the key (that is, the more bits it takes up), the stronger the encryption is. Theoretically, a 4096-bit key would be great. However, coding and decoding with long keys takes significantly longer (depending on the capacity of your PC). A 1024-bit or even 2048-bit key should be enough in most cases (2048 is the suggested default here, and also the default if you generate a key by not choosing the *Expert* option).

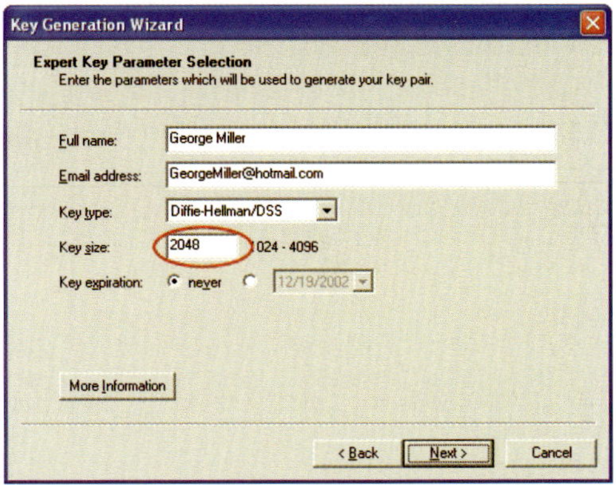

7 Next, you can determine for how long the keys are valid. Having an expiration date increases security, for even if someone were to crack your key, she could work with it for a limited time only. However, you also have the added hassle of having to distribute the new public key to your correspondents every time the old key expires. In addition, after your key expires, you won't be able to decrypt messages encrypted with that key anymore. The additional effort thus rarely makes it worth having an expiration date for private correspondence. Choose *never* for *Key expiration* instead.

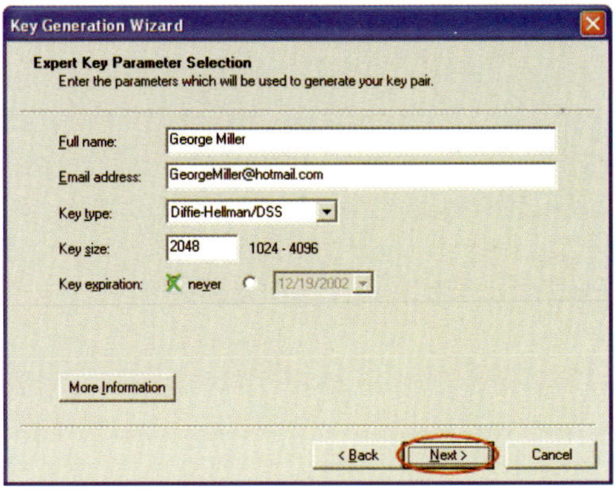

8 If you don't want any unauthorized person to work with your key, you need to protect it with a password, which you can enter in the *Passphrase* field. The longer the password and the more special characters it contains, and so on, the more secure it is. The *Passphrase Quality* meter shows you how secure your password is. To ensure that you haven't entered the wrong password by mistake, enter it again in the *Confirm* field. (For security reasons, it is not possible to select, copy, and insert in these fields.) Should someone be looking over your shoulder while you are entering this information, enable *Hide Typing* to hide all characters while you type.

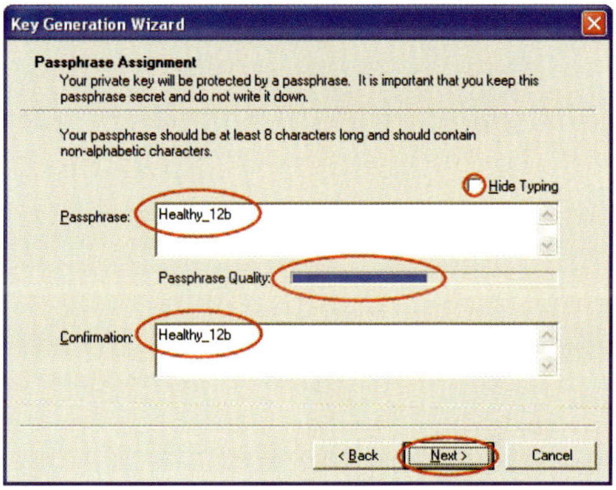

9 PGP then creates the keys.

10 Once you have finished generating a key with the wizard, you are back in the main program. It is possible that someone distrusts your public key, for it could be forged. For this reason, you should try to get the key to the user in as many different ways as possible. One way is the PGP public key server, on which you can leave your key. When someone needs your key, she either turns to you, and you send her the key, or she goes directly to the server. If you want to offer this convenience (you can always do it later), connect to the Internet now by right-clicking the key and going to *Send to* in the pop-up menu that appears. Select a server to transfer the key to; PGP accesses it and transfers the data.

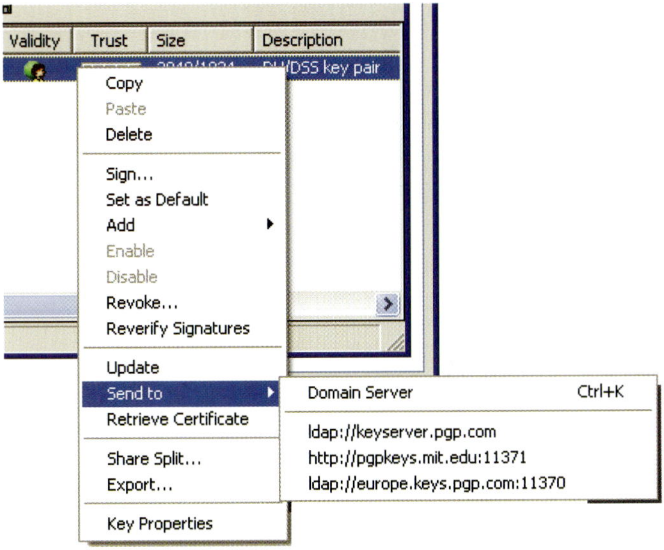

11 Your new key is displayed in the PGPkeys program. When you close PGPkeys, the program reminds you that the key you just created is of enormous importance and you should therefore create a backup key. Click *Save Backup Now* to save your public key (*Pubring.pkr*) and then your private key (*Secring.skr*). For security reasons, you shouldn't save the keys to the hard drive but on two separate diskettes.

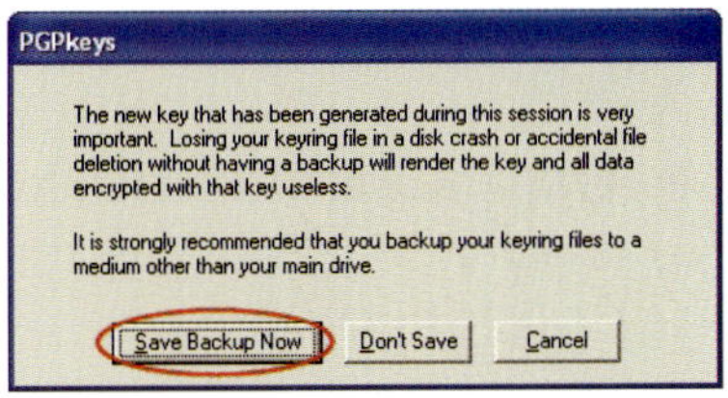

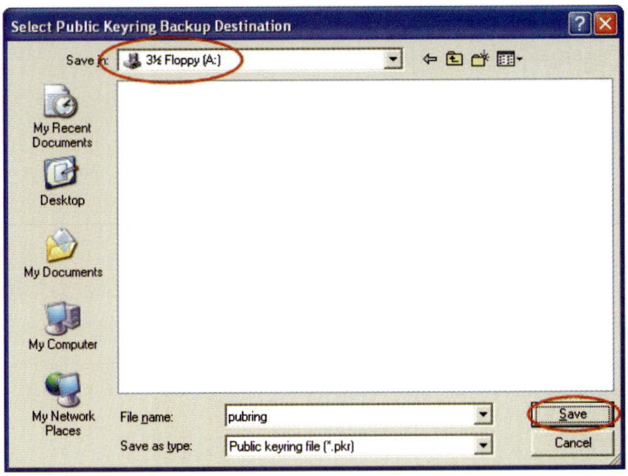

Before you start, you need to exchange keys

Now that you have created your PGP keys, you can start signing your e-mails. And then what? The e-mail recipient won't be able to verify the authenticity of your signature without your public key. And you can't encrypt any messages yet, because you need the recipient's public one for that. So you'll have to exchange keys first:

1 Start PGPkeys to export your public key. Select the entry for the desired key by clicking it.

2 Go to the *Keys/Export* menu to open the dialog box for saving.

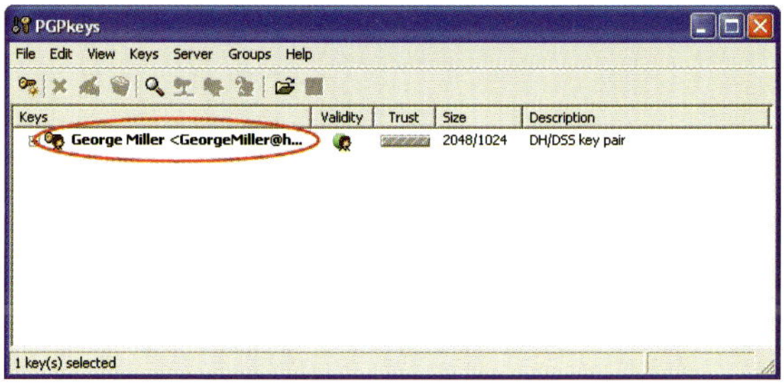

3 Select a target path and file name as usual. PGP proposes a name, but it often doesn't make much sense. You should select a name that is generally valid and works with every operating system, especially if you want to distribute your key to many people. This means that you shouldn't use any special characters, like diacritics and spaces, or more than eight characters. Do not enable the option *Include Private (Key)s* for any reason; otherwise, your private key is also saved, and the recipient could misuse it!

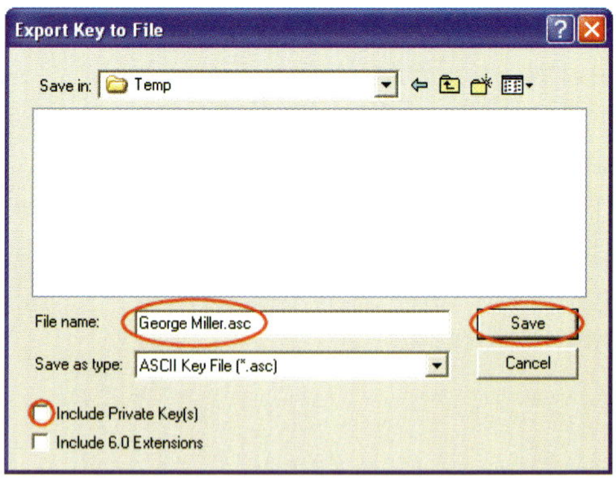

4 The key (in the illustration, the public key in the text editor) is saved like a normal text file (*.asc*) that can be distributed in many different ways.

Imagine someone writes an e-mail and pretends he's you. He even signs the e-mail, and the recipient, after verifying the signature, believes that everything is okay and that you have really written the message. This is easy to do and represents the only weakness of the public key system. The forger only needs to create a key ring with your data and to distribute the public key in your name. If you don't want this to happen, distribute the public key you have just exported by as many means as possible:

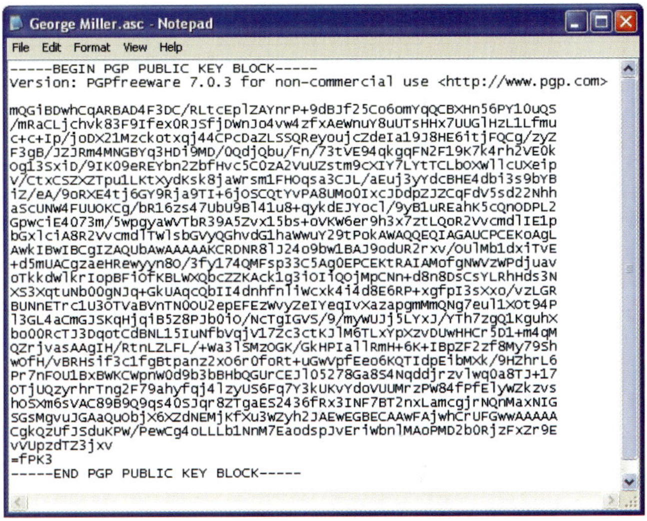

Use the PGP key server.

- Give your acquaintances a diskette with the ASC file for your key. This is the safest method!
- Send all your acquaintances an e-mail with your public key.
- Publish the key on your Web page.
- Send a fax with the content of your ASC text file.

This way, your correspondents can compare the several keys they have received and verify their authenticity.

When you receive a public key, you must import it into PGP to encrypt the message.

1 If PGP is installed on your computer, you only need to double-click the file name in Explorer. PGPkeys opens and imports the file.

2 Simply select only the key(s) you want to import and click *Import*.

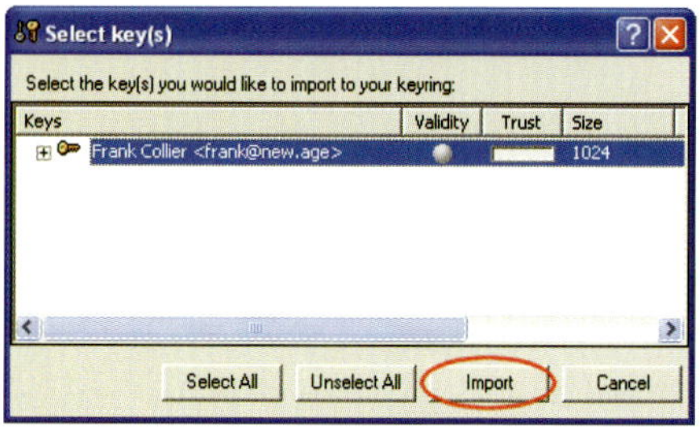

3 As an alternative, you can start PGPkeys and select the file of the key you want to import by going to the *Keys/Import* menu.

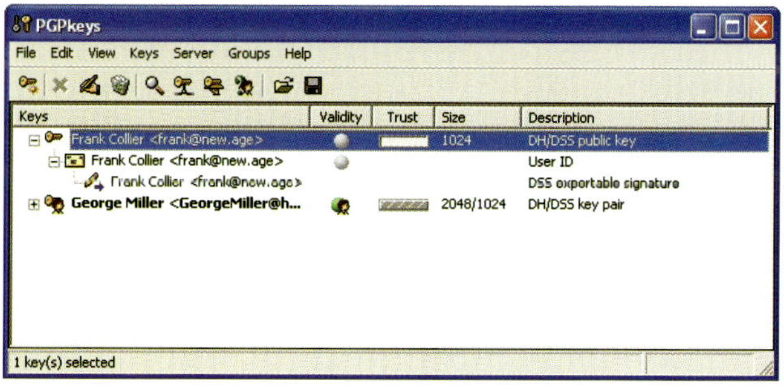

To get a public key from the PGP key server, you can use a special function for when you want to encrypt a message but don't yet possess the public key of the recipient:

1 Start PGPkeys and select the menu *Server/Search*.

2 Leave the default server selection and enter the name of the person whose key you want into the text entry field. If necessary, you can change the search terms for the list boxes that now read *User ID* and *contains*.

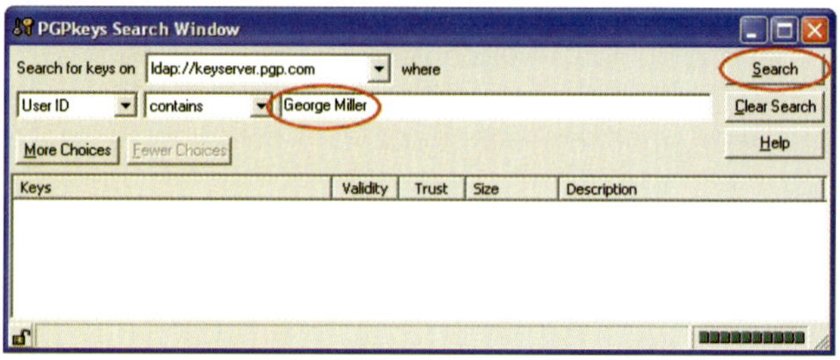

3 Connect to the Internet and start the search by *Search*.

4 After a few moments, the keys matching your query are displayed. Browse the list and select the desired key by clicking it.

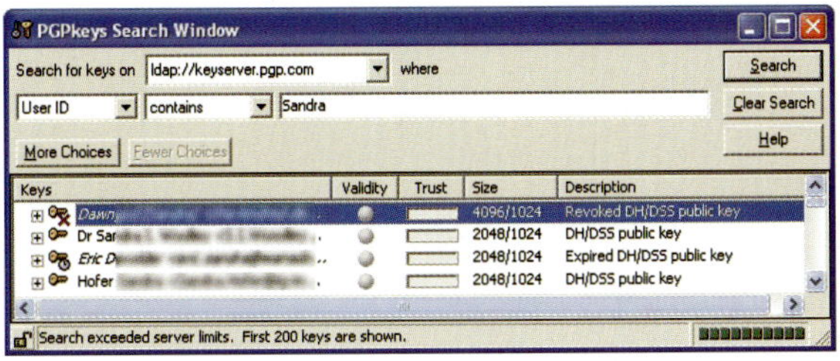

5 Right-click the selection to open the pop-up menu. Select *Import to Local Keyring* to add the key to your key ring, so you can use it any time in the future.

Even though you have now imported a key, you still can't use it. For your own protection, PGP automatically assumes that every key is forged. Your next step is to sign the key and confirm that you trust it.

1 Select the new key by clicking it and open the menu *Keys/Properties*.

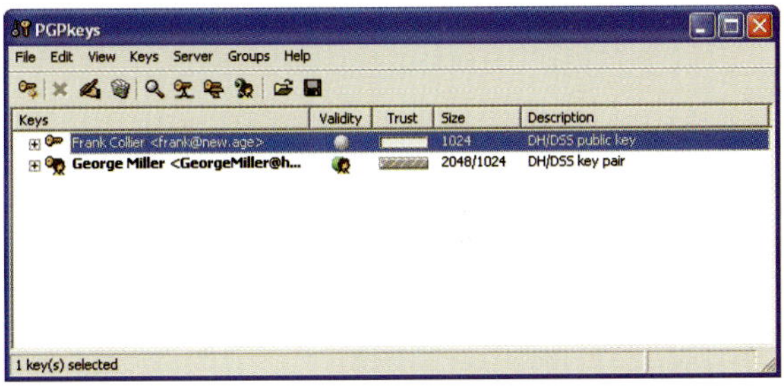

2 Now, you and the owner of the key must verify together if you have received the authentic public key. To avoid going through the entire length of the key to compare it, PGP creates a fingerprint of the key. The fingerprint is easier to compare and ensures that you have the right key. You can either compare the word list under *Fingerprint*, or enable *Hexadecimal* and compare the visible hex values.

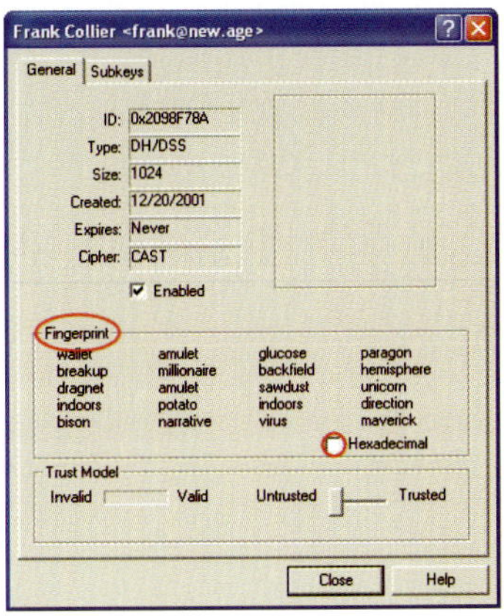

To compare the fingerprint, proceed as you would when exchanging keys: call the owner and let him send you a letter or fax. The owner might have even provided a fingerprint on his Web page.

> **Note**
>
> **Don't become irresponsible**
>
> Even if the procedure detailed above seems somewhat tiresome and you could leave out the comparison of the fingerprint, you shouldn't grow careless. A forged key can cause big mischief if you trust it without verifying it.

If you have compared the fingerprint and everything's OK, close the dialog box and sign the key with your own:

1 Select the key you obtained once again, if necessary, and go to *Keys/Sign*.

2 If you have verified the authenticity of the key in the previous step, you can sign the key with *OK*.

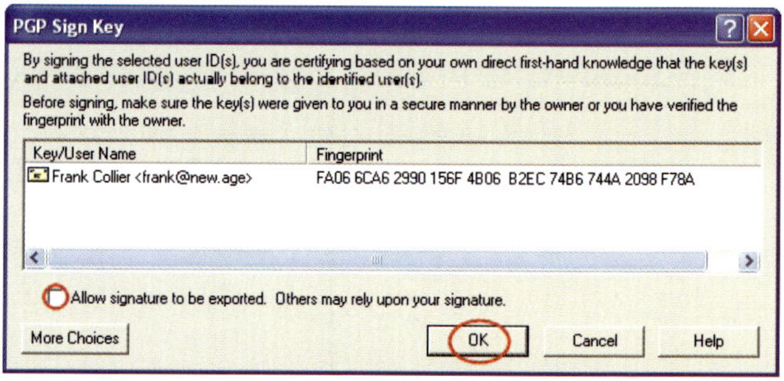

If you enable *Allow signature to be exported*, your signature is exported when you next establish contact to the PGP key server. Other people who want to use the key see that you trust it, and if they trust you, they don't have to verify the key on their own. This principle is effective.

3 To complete the signature, you only need to enter the password for your private key.

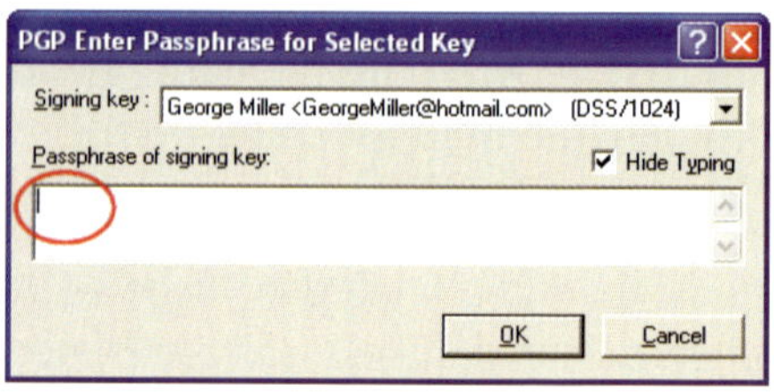

4 Leave the key you have just signed selected, and re-open *Keys/Properties*. Because you have signed the key, you can move the scrollbar to *Trusted*.

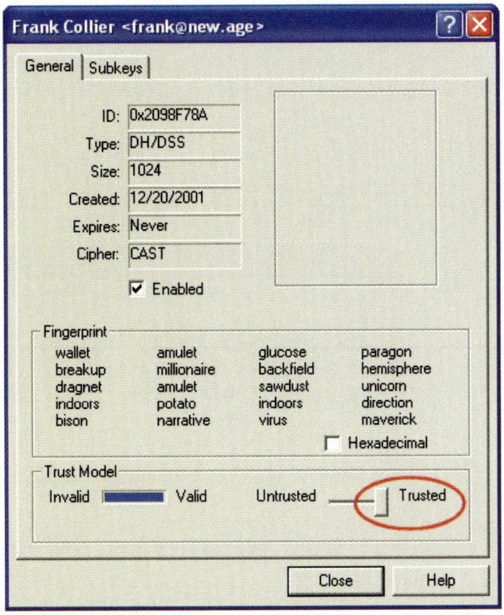

5 PGPkeys marks valid keys with a green dot. Your signature with the pencil icon confirms the authenticity and the bar filled in gray under *Trust* expresses your trust. Now you can safely exchange confidential information with the owner of the key.

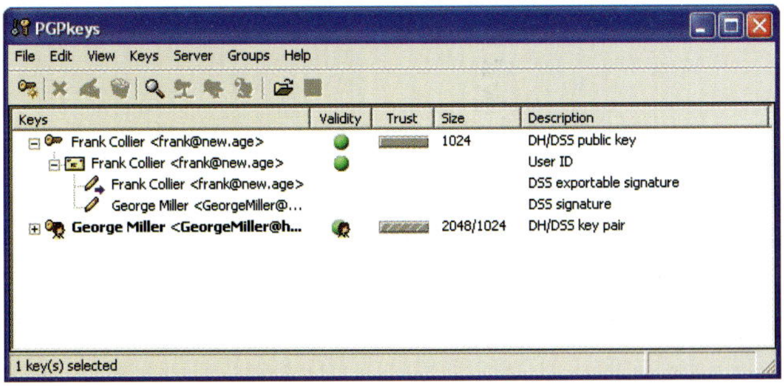

Using PGP for e-mails

No matter which e-mail program you use, you can always use PGP. In fact, you can use it even when you want to encrypt plain text instead of e-mails. During setup, PGP even installs corresponding plug-ins for Outlook and Eudora. Using PGP with these e-mail programs thus becomes still easier. You want to compose and then sign and/or encrypt an e-mail? First, compose the message in your e-mail program as usual.

Composing an e-mail in Eudora:

1 Create the e-mail you want to encrypt.

2 In Eudora, you can determine whether you want to encrypt or sign the message by clicking one of two additional buttons. After making your selection, click *Send*.

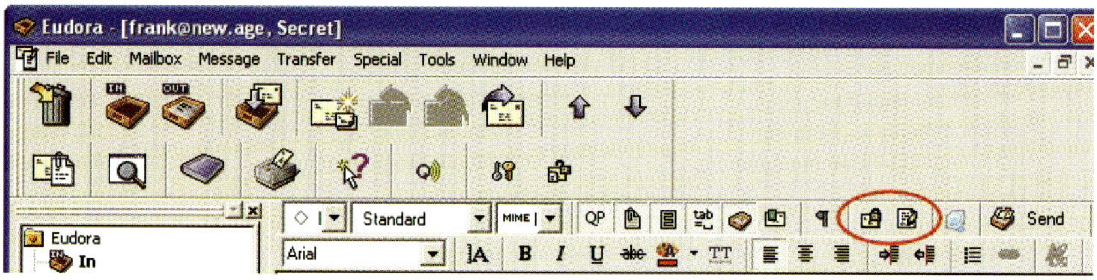

3 To sign a message, select the private key with which you want to sign it (usually, one of your own), and enter the corresponding password.

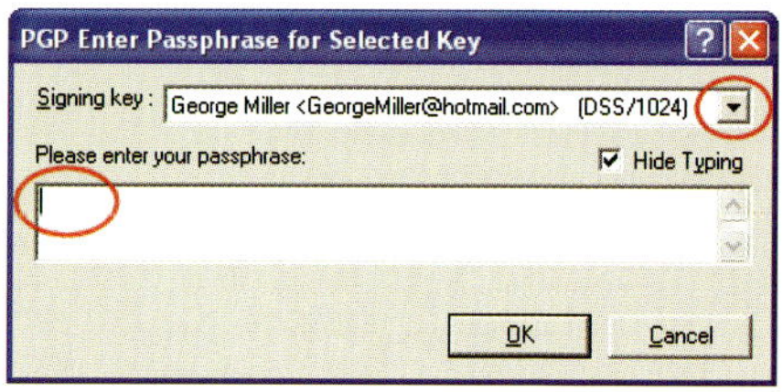

4 If you want to encrypt a message, you must first determine the recipient. Drag the recipient's name from the list at the top to the one below, for PGP to use the corresponding public key. If PGP recognizes the recipient of the e-mail by the information entered in the *To* field, this step is left out, and the e-mail is encrypted automatically.

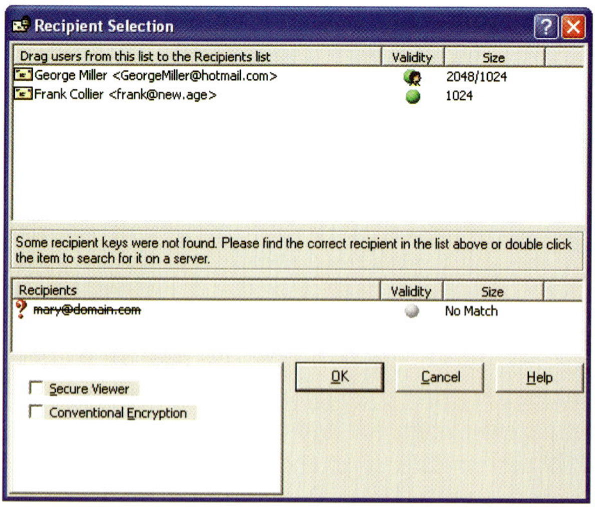

5 Whether you have encrypted or signed the message, it is now displayed in Eudora's Outbox but without its content.

6 When you receive a PGP message, Eudora announces whether the e-mail is signed or encrypted. If the message is signed, you can see the text. A message box informs you if the signature is valid. If the message is encrypted, you see cipher text, as in the illustration. To decrypt it, you first must open the message in a separate window by double-clicking it. Don't forget to keep your password handy for the decryption; only then can you read the e-mail and save any file attachments.

Using PGP with Outlook is as easy as with Eudora:

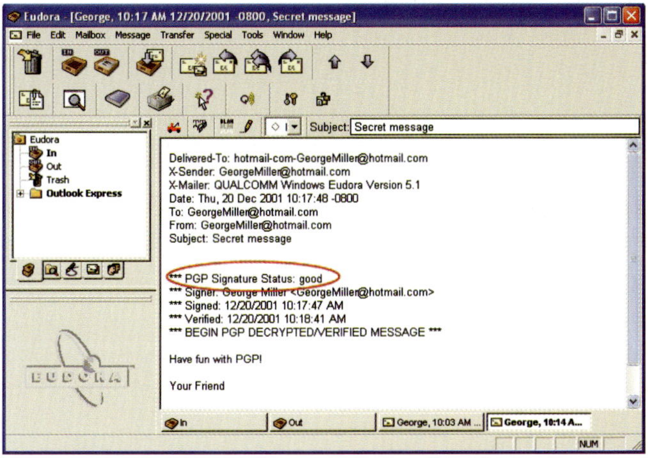

3. Signed and sealed: Secure e-mails

1 Compose an e-mail as usual. Afterwards, click the two additional icons to encrypt and/or sign the message.

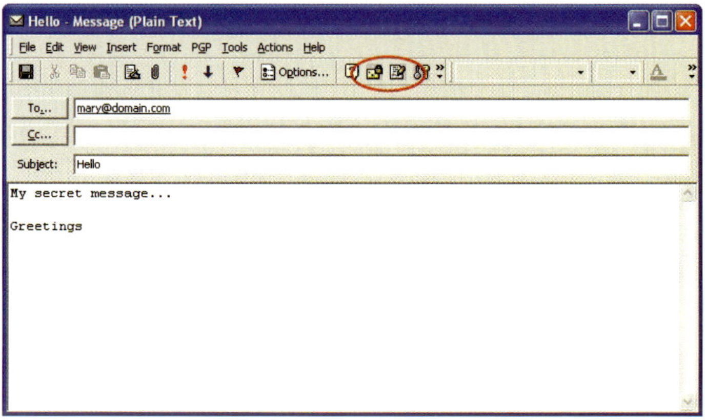

2 Click *Send*. You are then prompted to enter your password to sign the message or select the public key of the recipient (if the program doesn't recognize the recipient entered under *To*; compare steps 2 and 3 for Eudora).

3 You can view the messages in the Outbox as usual.

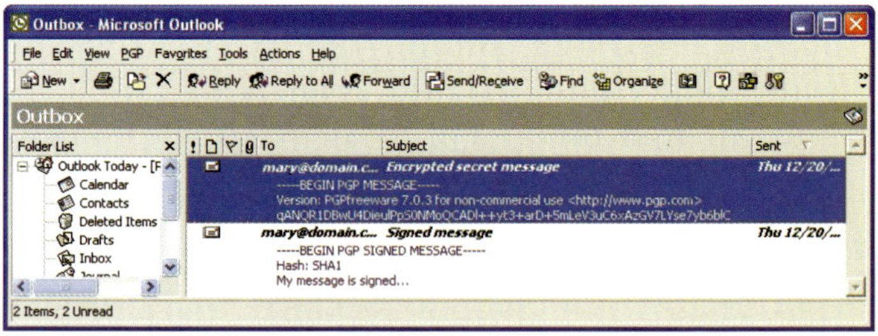

4 For received e-mails that were encrypted or signed with PGP, Outlook displays the text of the message as it was sent out. In signed messages, the text is located between commentary lines, and the digital signature is located at the bottom in the form of a row of characters. Encrypted messages are made up of random characters with no direct relation to the text or its length.

5 To read the message or verify the authenticity of the signature, open the message in a separate window by double-clicking it. Click the PGP lock icon at the top edge of the window. In the dialog box that opens, enter your password for your private key.

Note

What should you do if no PGP icons are displayed?

Even if your e-mail program doesn't support PGP plug-ins, you can still use the same features: create your e-mail and leave the text window open. Click the PGP icon in the tray bar and select the desired function from the *Current Window* menu. The content of the current window is then encrypted.

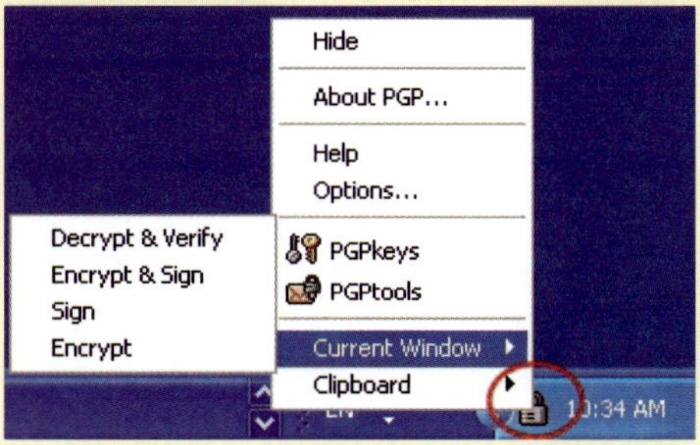

4. Protect yourself against vermin

Danger while surfing is not only lurking in the form of attacks by people wanting to spy on your computer. Even after you have long broken the connection to the Net, you can experience nasty surprises. While you have cast out your net across the Web looking for the latest drivers, and so forth, a few unwanted fish have also entered into your net and are attacking your system or, if harmless, are annoying you.

Viruses, Trojans, hoaxes, and other unwanted tenants

In the computer realm, all harmful programs performing tasks that are of no use are considered viruses. Viruses get onto your computer in various hidden ways. Previously, viruses were transmitted mainly through diskettes and pirated copies, but nowadays, the Internet is their breeding ground.

What is a virus?

A virus has several properties:

- It attacks a system and hides itself from the user.
- It copies itself on its own and spreads itself in various ways, for example, through diskettes or the Internet.
- It can do damage to your system in various ways: it can delete or make files unusable, or simply permanently display dialog boxes or something similar, hindering your work.

Note

Hardware cannot be damaged

Rumors are always circulating that viruses can also damage hardware. That is nonsense. Hardware can never be damaged. The only known virus that goes in this direction erases the BIOS in the EEPROM on the motherboard, but by doing so it is only damaging software - although that is definitely annoying.

Viruses appear in many different forms, of which several important basic types are usually just varied. Viruses all have something in common: they must be implemented; the pure virus file is harmless.

- **Boot block viruses** (also Master Boot Record or MBR viruses) nest themselves in the starting region of a hard drive or diskette. Each time when you start your computer, the boot block is read, and the virus is started.
- **File viruses** (usually) attach themselves to an executable file such as **.exe* or **.com*, for example. The affected program can appear to function completely normally at first, so that you don't notice the affliction. However, the virus is executed each time the program is started and can thus spread undetected.
- **Macro viruses** have only become significant with the increasing circulation of MS Office. MS Office can be expanded through self-written programs. These programs are saved in a normal document and passed on. If such a document is opened, the virus is launched.

Most of the viruses found in circulation are built on the principles of old functions that are accessible to anyone on the WWW. New viruses can be created with little effort, and even complete programs are available for doing so. People who simply want to show off with their virus or test what is doable therefore bring many viruses into existence. How many viruses are in circulation at any given time is logged by the WildList, which assembles viruses spotted "in the wild". At http://www.wildlist.org/WildList you can also find the current virus dispatches.

Trojan horses and their hidden freeloaders

Remember the way in which Odysseus obtained victory over the Trojans through cunning? Modern spies operate in the same way: they mask themselves as useful programs and hope that you let them into your system and install them. Such Trojan horses (called "Trojans" for short) are primarily useful programs that you are happy to install. The negative properties of the program contained within only become active later or are hidden. What happens then can be very complex: several Trojans gather information which they then send home to their creators; others open your system's back doors, through which attacks are made possible.

One member of this guild is Back Orifice, which belongs to the group "Cult of the Dead Cow". This free program that you can find at the Web site http://www.bo2k.net actually serves as a tool for remote maintenance among other things, similar to PCAnywhere and others. Once installed on a target computer, it can then be accessed from any other PC. The problem with this is that, for all intents and purposes, Back Orifice can be installed undetected and you know nothing of its existence, but your "foe" has full access to your information.

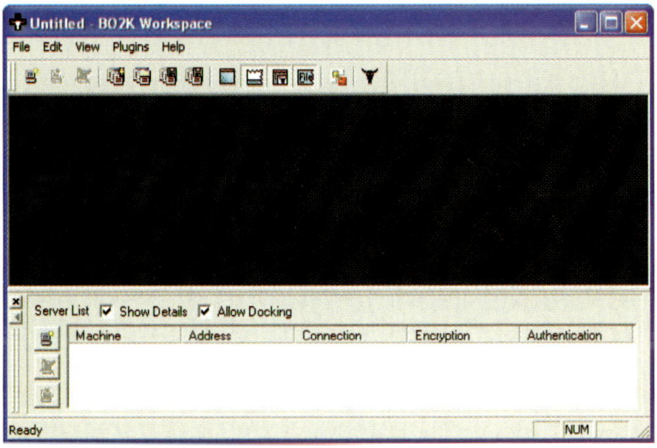

Modern virus scanners therefore also recognize Trojan horses and inform you with warning messages if you are about to install such a file.

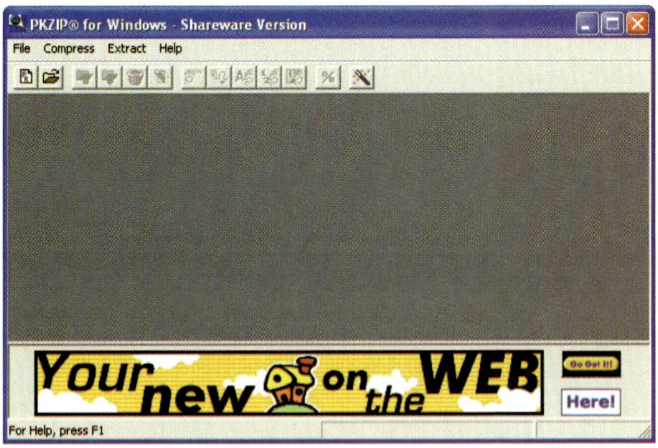

Programs such as TSAdBot also belong to the family of Trojans: they often attach themselves as an add-on to another program (often shareware) and nest themselves in the system of the unsuspecting user. The reasoning and purpose behind the whole thing is the financing of the software (in the illustration, software financed through advertising is spying on your computer; here, PKZip), for the installed robot then grabs ad banners from the Internet and displays them in the program window. It is actually not such a bad idea, except for a couple of snags:

- The robot is always working. Even if you are not using the ad-sponsored program, it wants to create an Internet connection and suck the data from the Net, whereby your hard drive gets filled up.
- You cannot get rid of it so easily again. Simply erasing the original program is not enough.
- Your PC can even be accessed from outside - as with Back Orifice - to delete data, spy out passwords or create user profiles, and so on.

The Radiate Web site also lists programs equipped with Radiate's ad banner under http://www.radiate.com/consumers/products.html.

To protect yourself from such programs, you must be especially careful when installing new software (particularly free software), carefully reading the details and not simply clicking them away, for the details about the ad robots are very well hidden.

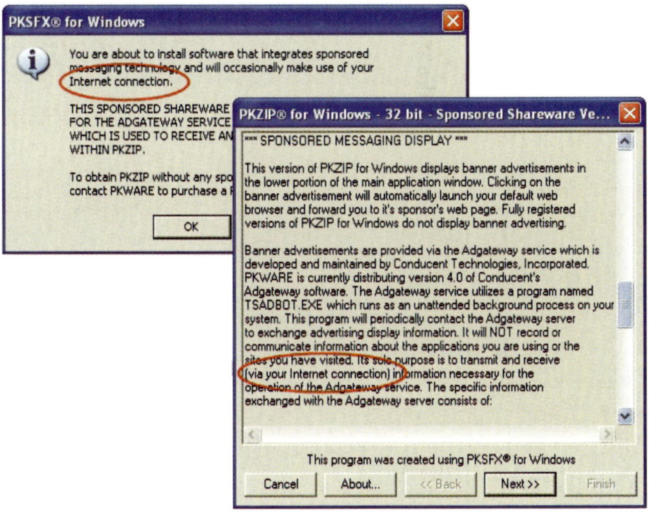

If the ad robot is already installed, it becomes a bit more of a task to get rid of it again. Excellent protection is offered by personal firewalls, which prevent the robots from accessing the Web (as described in the chapter about ZoneAlarm, starting on page 135), for they always recognize the activities of the robots and immediately alert you.

To identify and remove TSAdBot, proceed in the following way:

1 The directory *C:\Program Files\TimeSink* was created on your hard drive, in which the *TSAdBot.exe* can be found in the *AdGateway* subdirectory, giving the first clue to its existence.

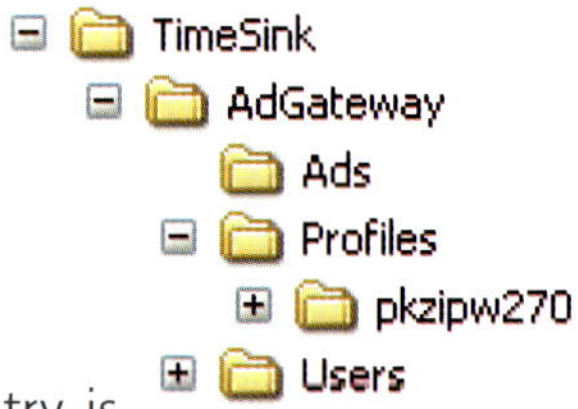

2 A further subdirectory, *Profiles*, contains, where applicable, its own subdirectory for each program that TSAdBot uses. This way, you can identify the critical programs.

3 In the key *HKEY_LOCAL_MACHINE\Software\Microsoft\Windows\CurrentVersion\Run* of the registry is an entry called *TimeSink Ad Client*. If you enter "regedit" in the *Start/Run* dialog window, the registry editor opens and you can click your way through it to the key.

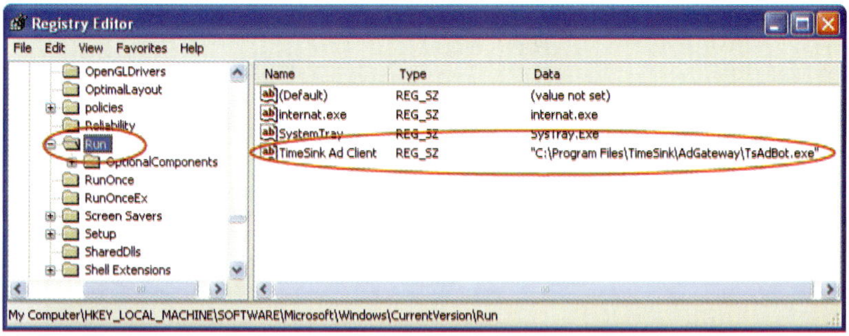

4 In the installation directory of each of the affected programs, you can find the file *TsUninst.exe*, with which you can prepare an end for the spook. To do so, you must go to the DOS interface (*Start/All Programs/Accessories/Command Prompt* in 2000/XP; *Start/Programs/Accessories/MS-DOS Prompt* in other versions), call up the program from the command line and use the parameter *-appname* and give the name of the burdened program: for example, *tsuninst -appname pkzipw* to remove it from PKZip (Program name *Pkzipw.exe*). However, you must repeat this procedure in each affected program directory. To completely clean the registry, you can manually search for the *tsadbot* entry and remove all the visible TimeSink keys.

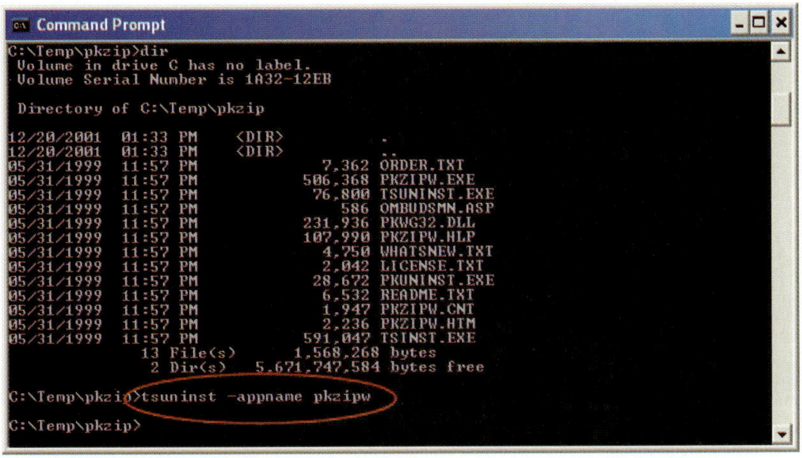

5 Alternatively, or additionally, you can erase the *C:\Program Files\TimeSink* directory. However, Windows denies this, because the program is still in use. Therefore, use a little trick: simply rename the directory with *File/Rename* in Explorer. Restart Windows, and you can now delete the folder.

The ad banner dummy from Radiate can be uninstalled in a similar way. An additional menu item might even exist in the Start menu. An uninstall done in this way, though, can possibly lead to the components installed by Radiate no longer functioning. With the alternative way, there shouldn't be any such problems:

1 In the *C:\Windows\System* folder you can find the file *Msipcsv.exe*. This is the wrongdoer that must be eradicated.

2 You can only delete the files in MS-DOS mode. In Windows 9x, you can switch to DOS by pressing the Ctrl key while Windows is booting up. You need an MS-DOS boot disk for Windows ME.

3 You can delete the file by entering *del c:\windows\system\msipcsv.exe* at the command prompt and restarting Windows.

```
C:\>del c:\windows\system\msipcsv.exe
```

Note

Yet more advertising

The Cydoor (http://www.cydoor.com) company also floods your PC with advertising (for example, in connection with their popular Babylon translator). To get rid of the ad Trojan, you must go to *HKEY_CURRENT_USER* and *HKEY_USERS*, *\Software\Microsoft\Windows\CurrentVersion\Run* in the registry, under the registry key *Cydoor*, as well as delete all other Cydoor entries. On the hard drive, the files *Cd_load.exe* and *Cd_client.dll* in the directory *C:\Windows\System* must be deleted (this is best done in MS-DOS mode, for the DLLs cannot be deleted from within Windows).

The Trojan test

Additional dangers presented by Trojan horses and programs that allow access to your computer can be discovered through a system check. Several Web sites offer you this service, testing your computer from outside for known points of attack. These tests search for open ports (the open doors for hackers), which are tested one after the other. An open port always presents a risk, because it means that data can be exchanged over it.

Note

A test is a targeted attack

In theory, a test always represents an attack, whereby all the ports are checked systematically (a port scan). The tester can misuse an open port upon its discovery and only appear to be informing you about security risks. Therefore, you should absolutely trust the Web site before using it. In addition, your provider might have something against this "attack". If need be, inform your provider about the test.

1 At http://www.anti-Trojan.net, you can perform this quick test for Trojans, which searches for known representative Trojans that use an Internet connection. Locate the link on the main page for the test.

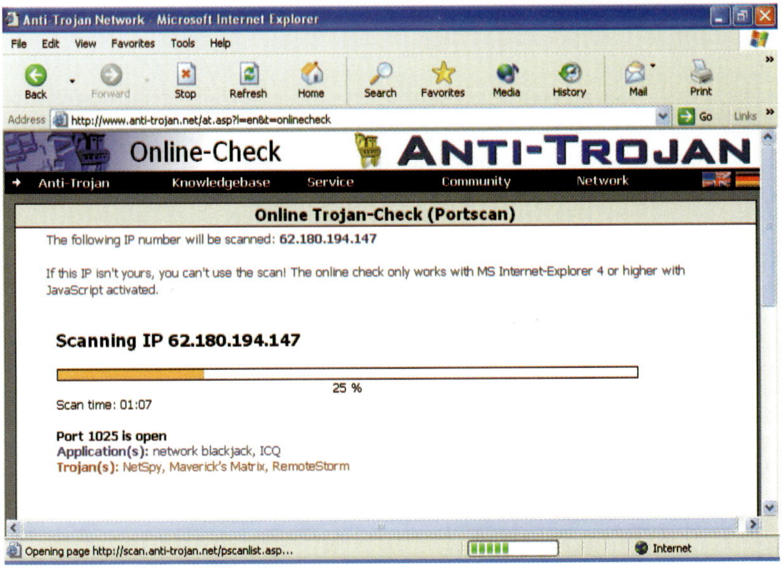

2 During the test, the status and which Trojans are currently being checked for are displayed. A status report then informs you about the possible dangers, and so forth.

Superfluous hoaxes

Hoaxes are false reports that spread themselves through e-mail and create a permanent nuisance. No real danger is presented by a hoax, for the message only spreads itself as a text dispatch. However, the financial expenditure for sending and so on can create enough damage, and massive amounts of hoaxes are annoying enough, just like spam, to want to do something about them.

4. Protect yourself against vermin

The content of the text (in the illustration, a typical representation of a hoax) is always somewhat similar: some large company or institution is supposedly planning a wonderful special offer and is calling the Internet community to join in it. So that you can belong to the group of lucky and good people, you should forward the e-mail to many people in addition to a particular person.

Afterwards, you receive a present, or a sum of money that is put into a charitable savings account, or something just as absurd. The whole thing is reminiscent of the long known chain letter, which of course also exists as a hoax and uses the deprivation of love or long lasting misery as a threat, if the chain is broken.

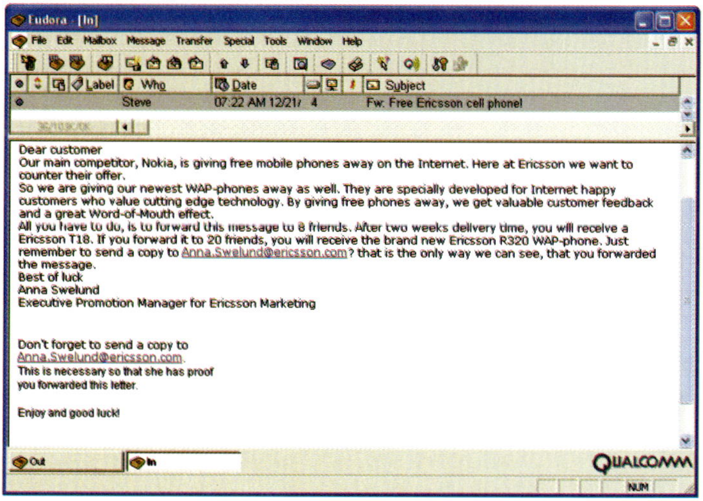

Hoaxes are annoying, and some of them are around for years, for some people always fall for untrue virus warnings and more. Above everything else, it is aggravating when your name always appears in the list of people to whom the letter should be forwarded to, for you can then expect to receive a flood of messages.

At http://www.ericsson.com, Ericsson provides a link to a page with denounces the hoax e-mail (see previous illustration).

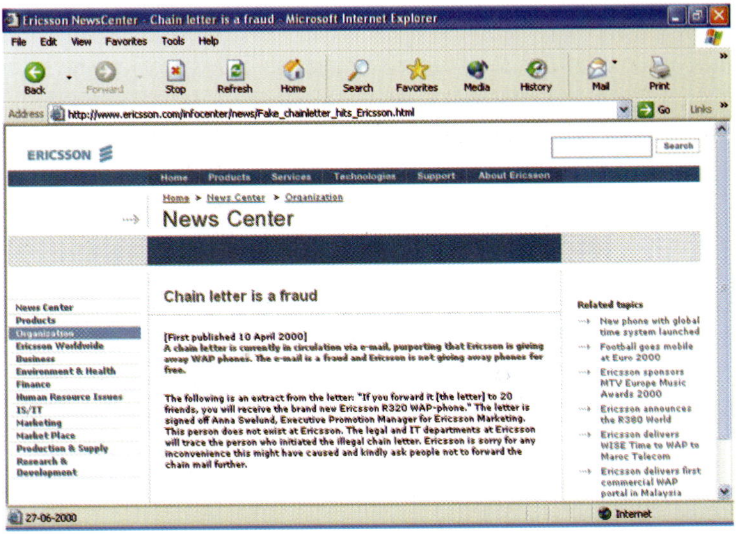

You can generally recognize a hoax by using common sense and by recognizing that you are requested to forward the message to as many acquaintances as possible. Always ask yourself why the company named would do this and what the purpose of the whole thing is. In addition, you can usually find a relevant notice that you are dealing with a untrue message on the Web site of the company in question.

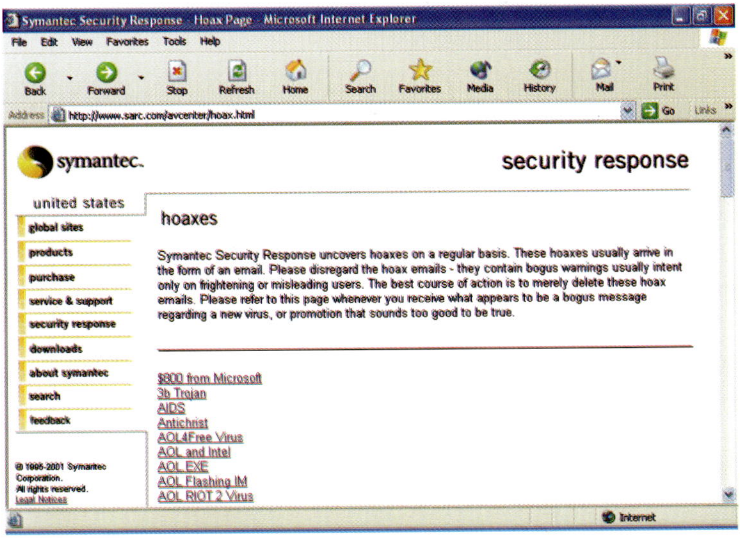

On the Web site http://www.sarc.com/avcenter/hoax.html you can find considerably more information about hoaxes and a list of examples from known chain letters. If you come across a new hoax, you can send in your discovery by e-mail, so that other users can be warned about it. Otherwise, the only correct way to deal with it is to delete it.

When your software is leading a secret life: Spyware

What would you think if your graphics program or some other software were quietly and furtively collecting information about you and then sending it at the right opportunity to its creator through the Internet? The kind of information concerned can vary quite a bit: your name and the operating system used are still the harmless variations. But how about a complete list of all the installed software and license numbers or your bank information, or, or, or? Recently, this trend seems to be emerging more often.

After the Internet provider MSN unpleasantly stood out during its launch several years ago for practicing this, more and more software manufacturers are now using this trick to spy on users and in this way protect themselves from illegal copying, among other things.

True protection from such practices can only be offered by a firewall (see page 135), because it always informs you when software wants to send information over the Net.

Software from notable manufacturers that is installed on almost every system also belongs to the best-known representatives of spyware. RealPlayer or Microsoft's Media Player can collect information about the music played (whether it is taken from the Internet or exists locally on a CD or as an MP3) and the user. The data then gets sent to the manufacturer together with other user information. What interest the manufacturer has in this collection mania for its programs is obvious, the more so because its attitude has long been known and, up till now, neither a remedy for older program versions exists nor concrete advice for the user, unless it has been well hidden.

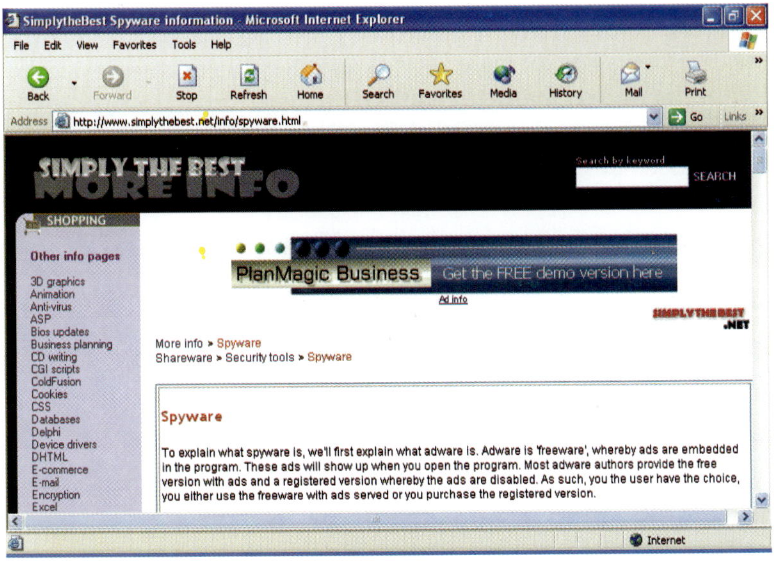

http://www.infoforce.qc.ca/spyware/

For the current version of Microsoft Media Player (here, version 7 with the Headspace skin), you can't stop the transfer of collected data - only a firewall (see page 135) is in a position to do so, but you can at least prevent meaningful recognition of your computer on the part of Microsoft or others, and protect your music files from being accessed by others.

1 Start the Media Player and go to *Tools/Options* (or right-click and select the *Options* entry from the context menu).

2 In the Player tab, find the *Allow Internet sites to uniquely identify your Player* option, which you can disable.

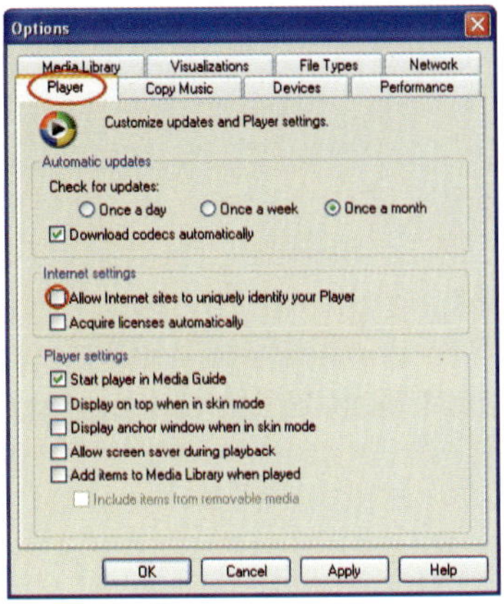

3 Because you're already at it, you can at the same time opt for more security by going to the *Media Library* tab and selecting the two *No access* options. Otherwise, other applications or Internet sites are given access to the files you have compiled in your Media Library. Or do you want all Internet users to help themselves to your PC?

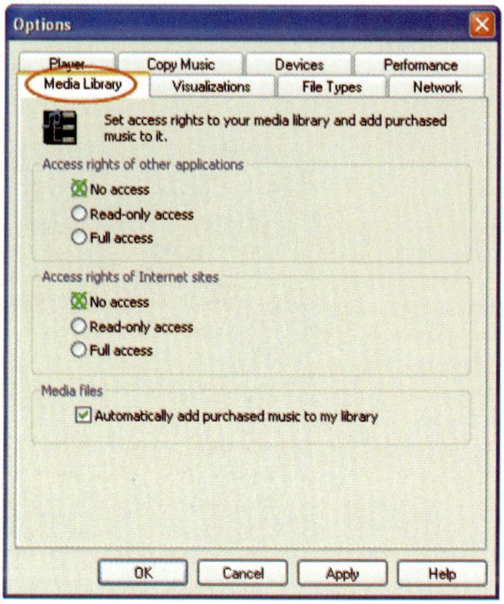

Plug-in terrorism with mouse pointers

The company Comet Systems (http://www.cometsystems.com) advertises "**FREE**, powerful and fun software for personalizing your mouse pointer", which has been installed by "over 90 million Web surfers". Perhaps you have already had the debatable pleasure of experiencing this wonderful product on your own – presumably without choice. The advertised tool is a simple plug-in that permanently changes your mouse pointer and bothers users with blinking and colorful pictures instead of the usual pointing device. Allegedly, this is to the joy and edification of the user, although more likely to gain money for Comet Systems from parallel online advertising.

In itself, it might be completely irrelevant what the Comet Cursor does, for, if you don't want to have it, there's no reason why others shouldn't amuse themselves with it. However, contrary to usual practice, Comet Systems knows no mercy and installs the new mouse pointer unexpectedly more or less behind your back, and then bombards you not only with mouse pointers, but also with advertising that most likely doesn't interest you at all.

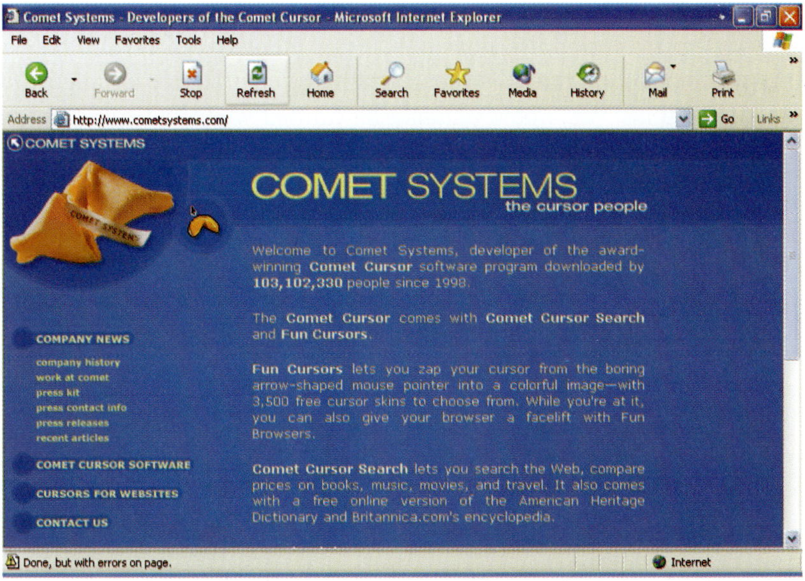

http://www.cometsystems.com

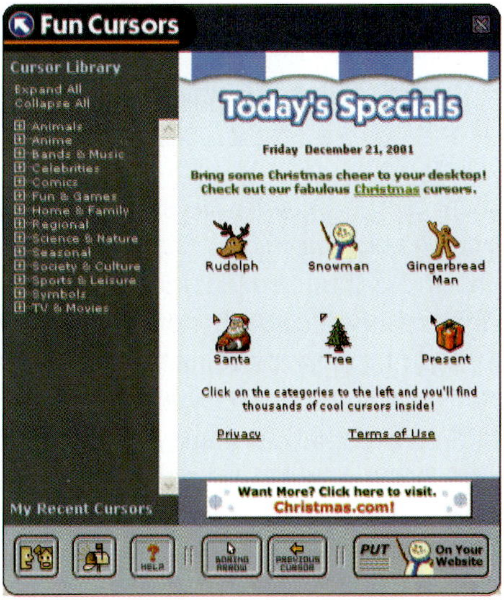

Particularly upsetting about the Comet Cursors is that you are generally not informed that the necessary program nests itself in your computer. You are merely visiting some Web site on the Net casting Comet Cursors left and right, and seconds later you need to find a solution to get rid of the annoying plague. To try out the technology, you only need to follow the link Comet Cursor Software.

Only a firewall (see page 135) can protect you from the nastiest perils and prevent the download of unwanted advertising images and mouse cursors. Especially because you don't know what information they are collecting on you and sending to Comet Systems.

ActiveX is to blame for the quick installation of Comer Cursor, which is why Netscape users are spared. They can only install an older version and only manually. In Internet Explorer on the other hand, the program is simply installed. With the right security settings, you would actually be warned when this takes place, for Comet Systems uses a signed ActiveX control for the installation.

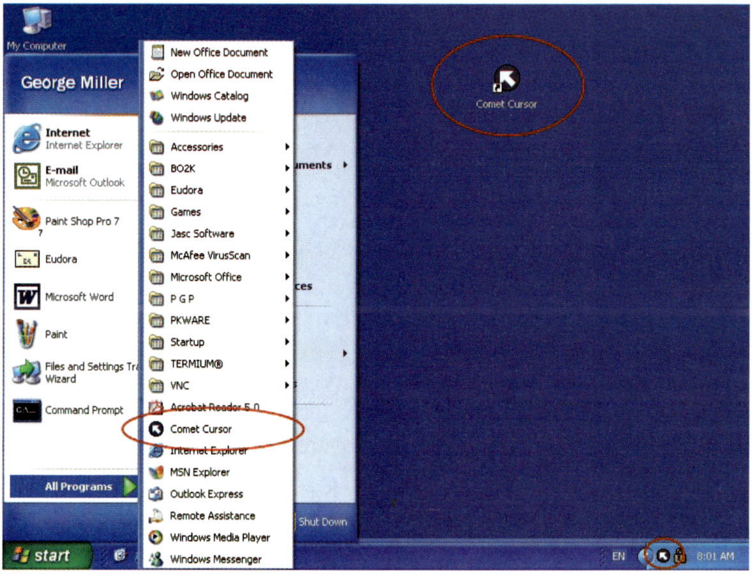

Go to *Tools/Internet Options/Security* and then to the *Security Settings* to determine how the browser should treat such controls. If you have selected *Disable* for *Download signed ActiveX controls*, nothing happens and Comet Cursor isn't a topic for you. Out of convenience, you most likely have chosen *Enable* or *Prompt*; otherwise, many Web sites do not work, and, in particular, online banking won't work without ActiveX. Generally, signed ActiveX controls are not dangerous – but what does danger mean? Your system does not always need to be immediately damaged.

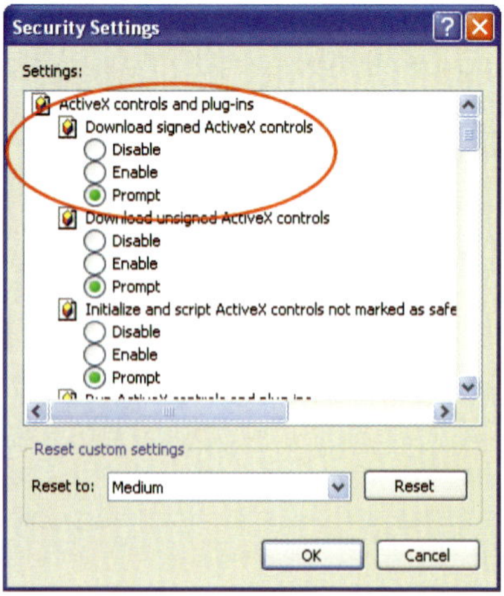

As demonstrated with the mouse cursors, the pure installation of software can already be unpleasant. The prompting does not yet protect you from the installation, for you usually do not pay particular attention to the certificate presented - especially because you cannot do much with the information and you cannot know what happens with your acknowledgement (the comments in the dialog window also give a false sense of security). Therefore, you click *Yes* out of habit, and you have already installed the program.

With the security warning you are most definitely warned, but a quick glance and a click for acknowledgement triggers the installation procedure:

If you have already been infected with the mouse pointers, it doesn't help to close the program by clicking the icon in the system tray, for it is active again the next time you start Windows. You must dig a little deeper into the bag of tricks:

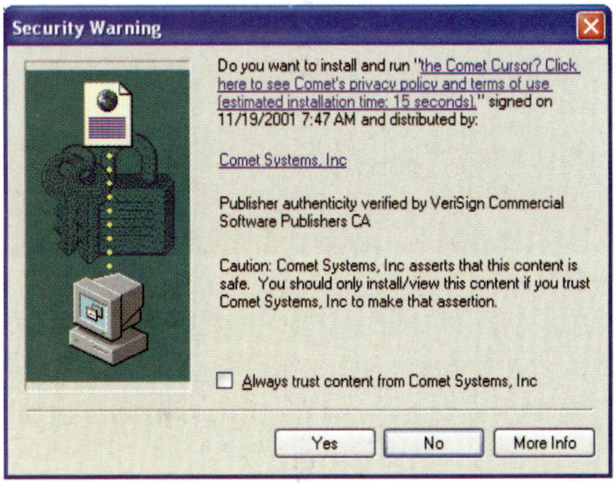

1 Go to *Add/Remove Programs* in the Control Panel (*Start/Settings/Control Panel*).

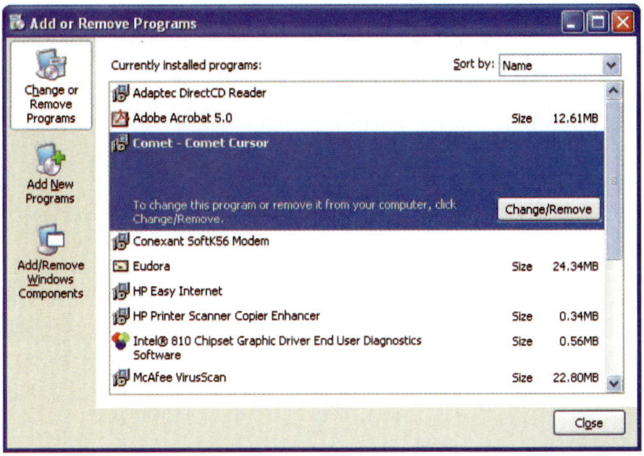

2 In the list of installed programs in the *Add/Remove Programs* tab, find the entrie(s) for *Comet*. If there are two entries, first click the second entry, *My Comet Cursor desktop application*.

3 With *Add/Remove*, you can delete this part of the program; to do so, you only need to confirm the dialog box that appears.

4 Afterwards, proceed with the other entry, *Comet Cursor Web browser extension*, in the same way. If there is only a single entry, delete it.

5 After restarting Windows afterwards, you are once again rid of this pest.

"I love you"? – VBS and Scripting Host

Until now, Trojan horses such as the I love you virus and Melissa have always used the same weak points on Windows computers: a **V**isual **B**asic **S**cript (VBS) is sent to a computer in an e-mail attachment; there, it executes and spreads further.

VBS was of course not primarily conceived for programming viruses, but to exhaust the computer's capabilities and create individual programs. As long as you don't belong to the guild of programmers and develop in VBS, you can do without Scripting Host, thus stuffing a blatant security gap, for, when the Scripting Host doesn't exist, VBS viruses don't have a chance.

1 The way to disable the Windows Scripting Host varies depending on the version of Windows you are using. If you are using Windows Me/2000/XP, simply open Windows Explorer, go to *Tools/Folder Options* and switch to the *Files* Types tab. Select the *VBScript Script File* entry and click *Delete.* If you are using Windows 98, the procedure is somewhat different. Go to the Control Panel (*Start/Settings/Control Panel*) and double-click *Add/Remove Programs*.

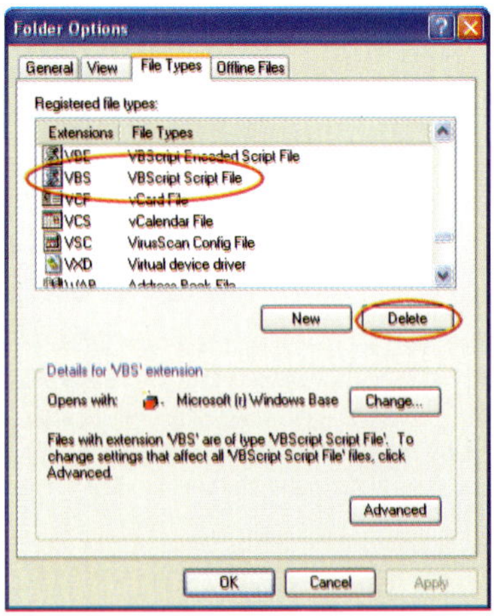

2 In the *Add/Remove Programs Properties* window switch to the second tab, *Windows Setup*, and look for the *Accessories* component. Double-clicking it brings you to the next dialog window.

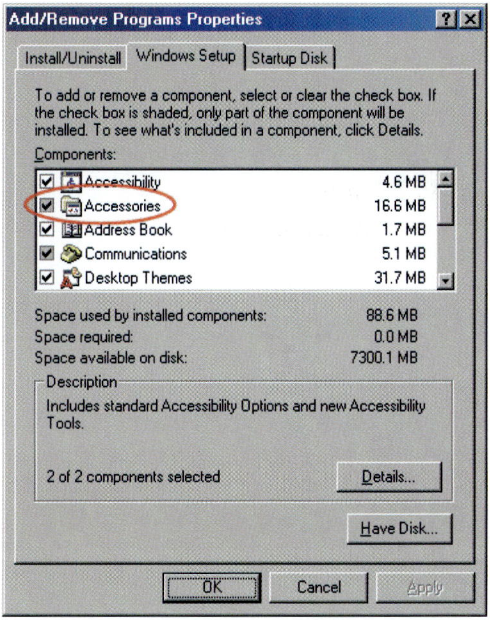

3 By removing the checkmark from in front of the *Windows Scripting Host* entry, you can remove the Scripting Host. Should you again need it later, you can after-install it at any time by re-enabling the option.

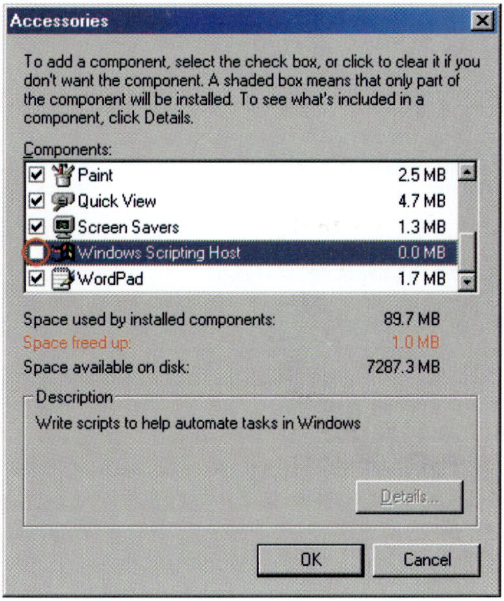

Virus scanners help

When were you sick last? Most likely, at the worst possible time. The same goes for your computer: when you need it most and expect it least, danger catches you off guard, and a nasty virus program clears your hard drive or makes every program crash.

You can effectively protect yourself against this type of infection with a virus scanner that permanently knocks off all files containing possible dangers and warns the user in each case. The danger of catching a virus is especially large when surfing the Net, because a large selection of free software is available for quick download, and the risk cannot be avoided.

Note

Microsoft affected by a Trojan horse

Even large corporations are not immune against viruses. As the Wall Street Journal reported in October 2000 (you can read about it in the Internet World News archive at http://www.internet-world.de/5tage_8588.html), the attack was likely made possible by the Trojan worm QAZ - already known since August - which was supposedly found in an e-mail attachment opened by a Microsoft employee. This way, hackers gained access to Microsoft's source code and could thereby change the code in such a way as to create backdoors in the products, which would lead to loss for users. The QAZ Trojan affects the Windows Editor *Notepad.exe* and can be easily recognized by the altered file size (120,320 bytes). Current virus scanners should have been able to warn against the Trojan, and it remains a mystery what exactly lead to such a breakdown at Microsoft.

Free virus scanners

In addition to the many commercial virus scanners for which you must pay, several free ones are available, such as AVG from Grisoft, for example. You can download the newest version of the nearly 5-MB file after entering some personal information at http://www.grisoft.com. You must definitely enter a place of residence in the USA; otherwise, you receive the demo version that you can recognize by the "us" in the file name. The necessary serial number is sent to you by e-mail.

The installation is relatively simple:

1 Start the setup by double-clicking the downloaded file *avg6286us.exe* in Explorer.

2 The first dialog windows with the Welcome message and the license agreement can be skipped by clicking *Setup*, *Next*, and *Yes* in that order. In the next dialog window, enter the serial number that was sent to you.

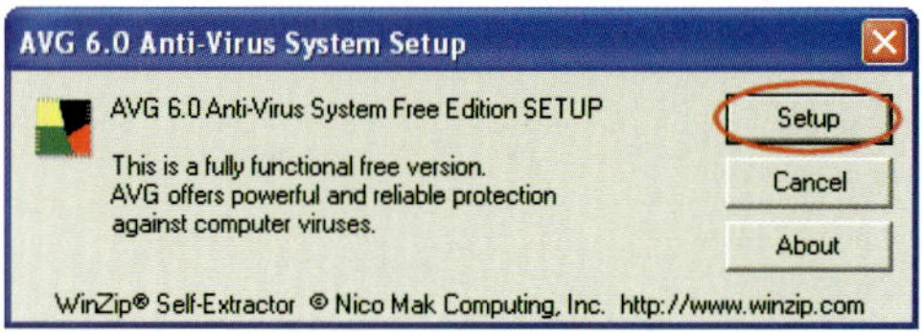

3 Determine the installation path, using *Browse* in the dialog window that follows or accept the recommendation. Confirm the installation summary that follows.

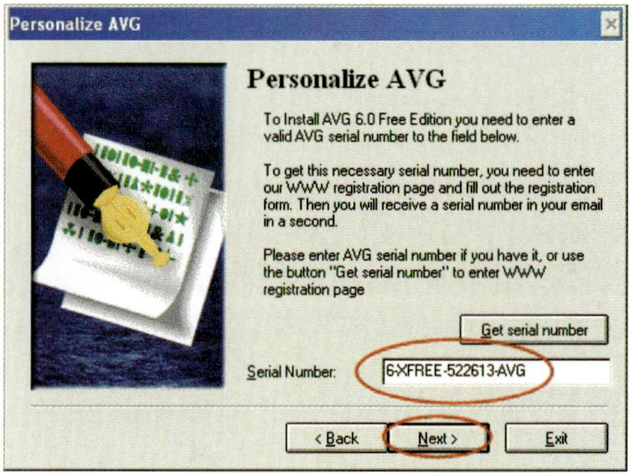

4 Select a Program Folder and start the copying process with *Next* and *Next* again in the window that follows with the summary of installation options.

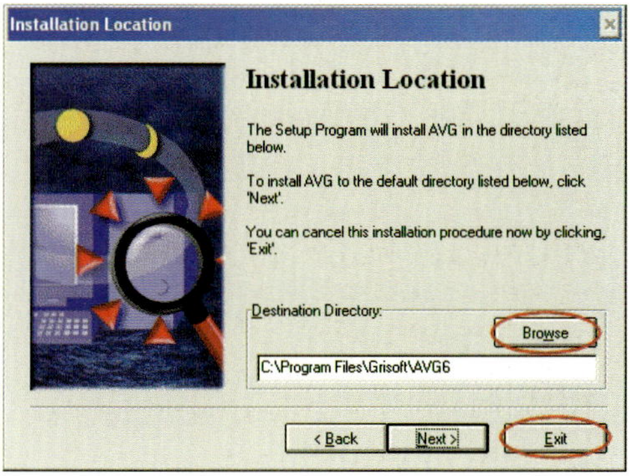

5 It's best to leave the recommended options in the configuration window.

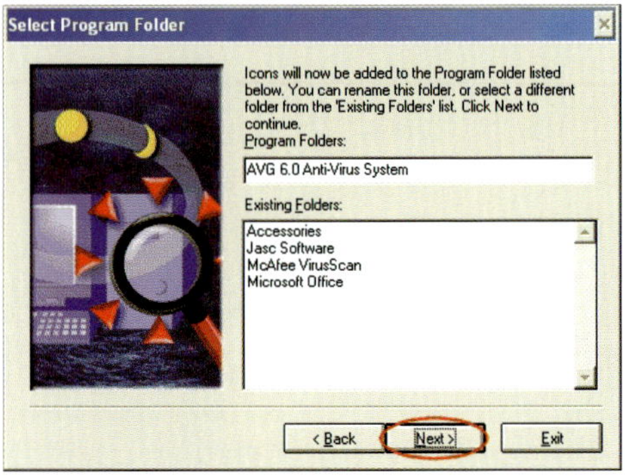

6 If you so desire, you can have the program automatically look for updates. This makes it more convenient for you, because you don't have to think about it, but at the same time, it presents a security hole, for the program has to send information into the Internet to do so. Decide for yourself what you prefer.

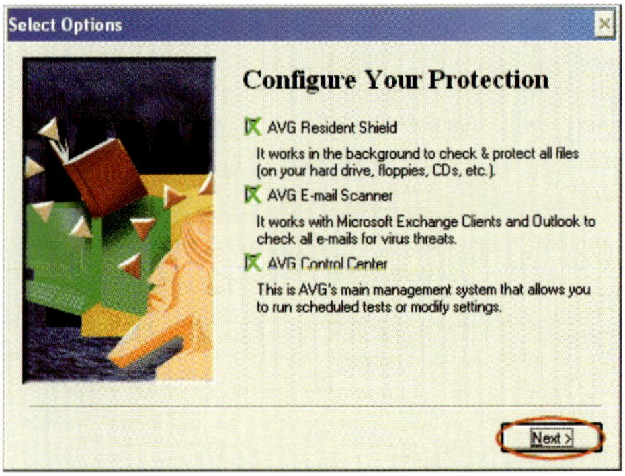

7 Afterwards, current information is displayed. You can disregard this and restart your system by clicking *OK*.

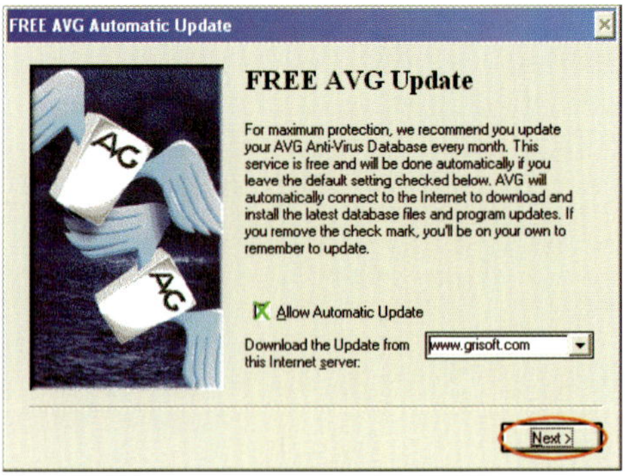

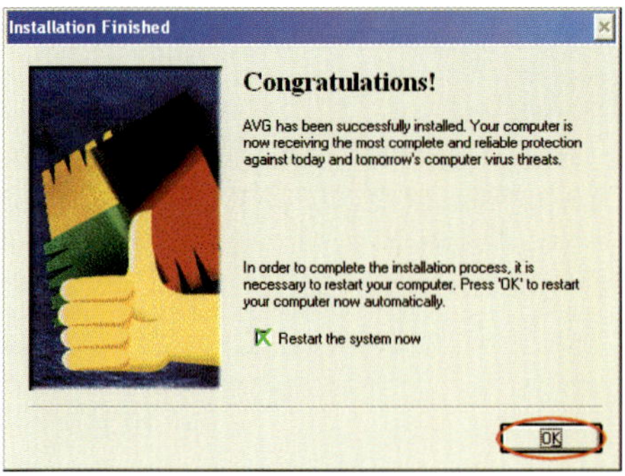

The first start-up

After you restart your computer, AVG starts up and greets you with the First Run Wizard.

1 Click *OK*.

2 The program would now like to update itself and to search for current virus information, which you can first bypass with *Skip Update*.

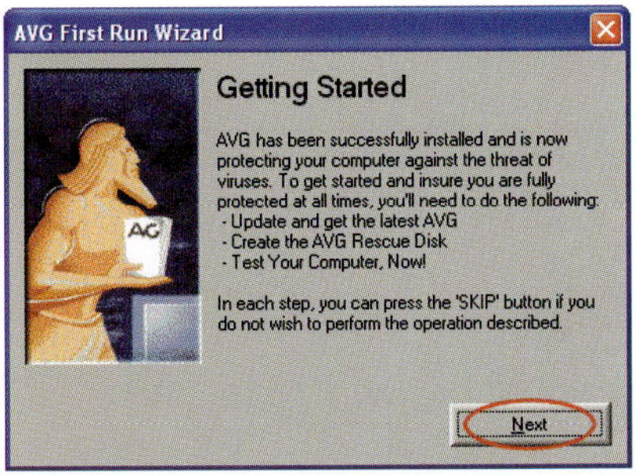

3 Afterwards, the program recommends you create a rescue disk, which is highly recommended. Click *Create Rescue Disk*.

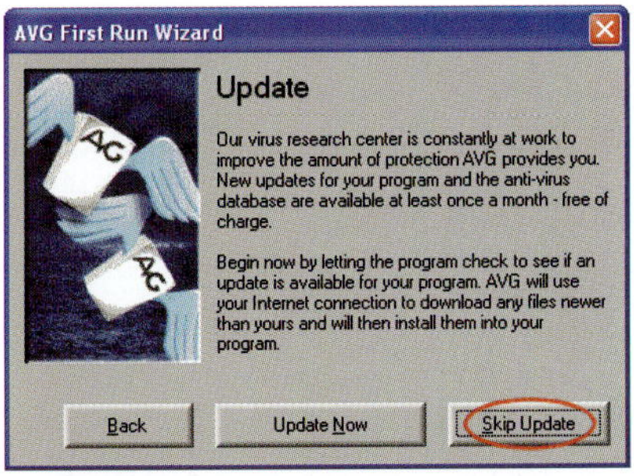

4 In the window that follows, reconfirm the creation of the disk. Insert a blank diskette, and in the next window, select the drive, if applicable. Continue by clicking *Create*.

5 To ensure that the disk is free from viruses, click *Format it*. Doing so deletes all the files on the diskette.

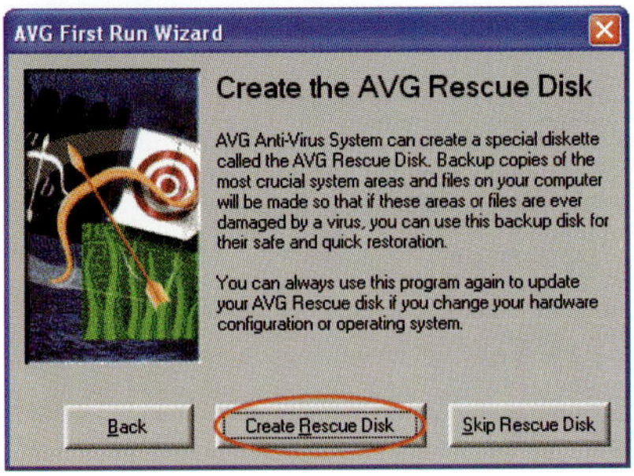

6 In the next window, you still must click *Start* to proceed, and, in the end, to close the summary. Back in the previous dialog window, click *Continue* to copy the files to the diskette.

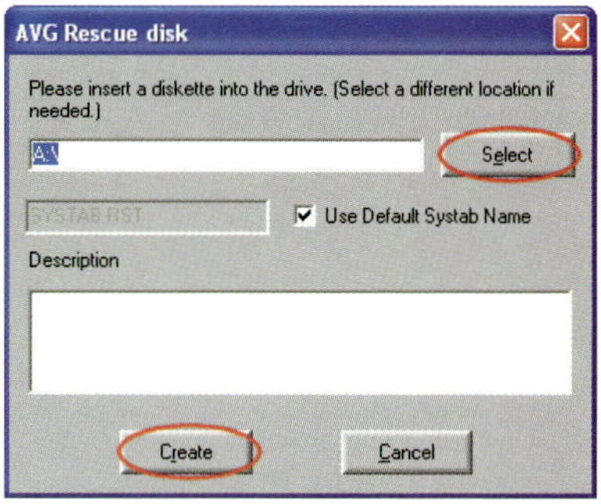

7 To rule out the possibility that you have a virus in your system, start the system test by clicking *Test Computer Now*, which shows you a summary upon completion.

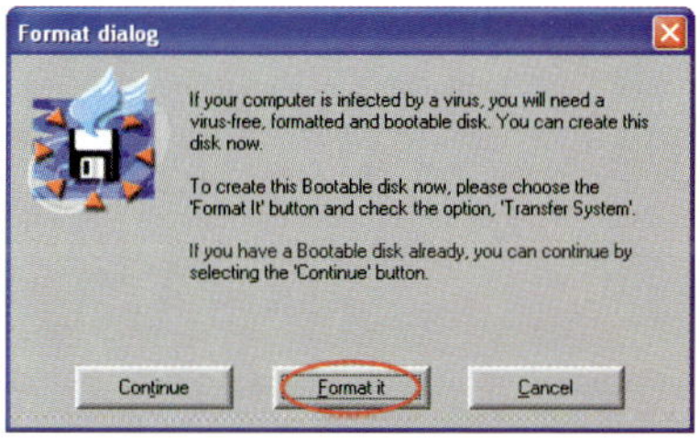

8 You are now finished and can exit the program by clicking *Exit AVG Now*.

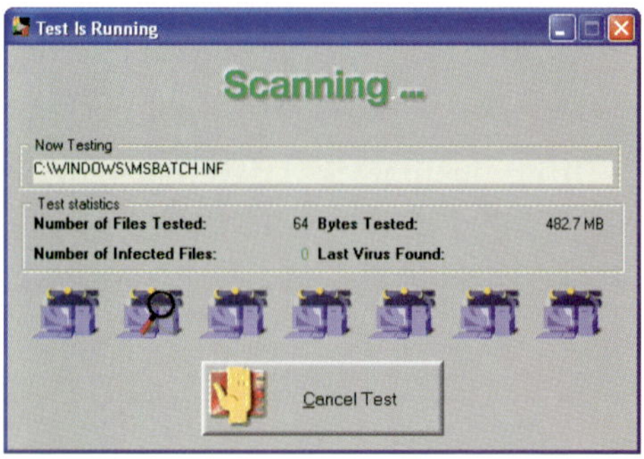

9 An icon in the system tray shows that AVG has been put into action and is henceforth monitoring your system. New files are now automatically checked for known viruses, and, if any danger lurks, the relevant warning is displayed.

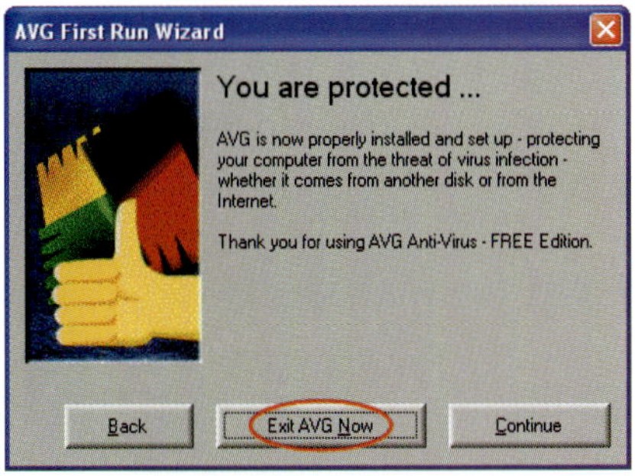

Virus scanners and Windows XP/ME

Under Windows XP/ME, your virus scanner has a somewhat difficult time mastering files potentially infested by viruses. This is because the Windows system restore function protects the system and makes it possible to recopy the files from a protected folder. Virus scanners are in a position to diagnose an infestation, but do not have any access to the write-protected system folder, so they cannot remove viruses. If your system is then repaired by means of the system restore function, the virus is once again spread. As long as Microsoft does not allow virus scanner manufacturers access to those types of files, the only possibility that remains is to disable the system restore function:

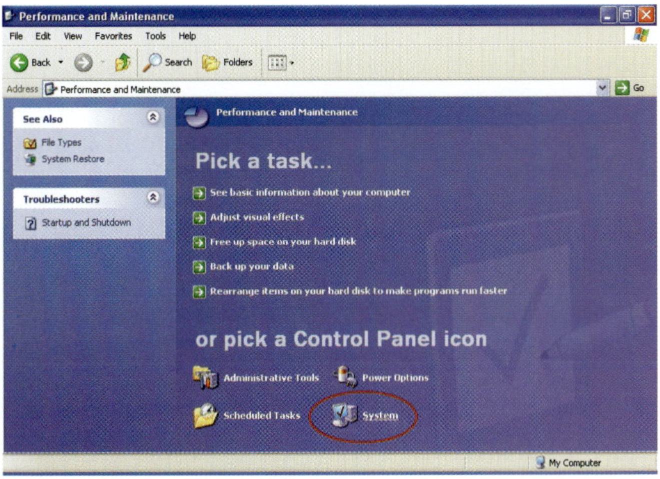

1 Go to the Control Panel and click the System icon (*Start/Control Panel/Performance and Maintenance* in XP; *Start/Settings/Control Panel* in ME) to open the *System Properties* window.

2 In XP, go to the *System Restore* tab; in ME, go to the *Performance* tab and click *File System*.

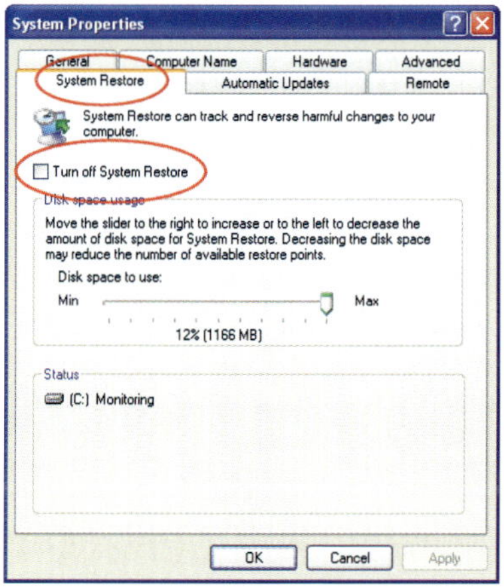

3 In XP, check the *Turn off System Restore* option; in the *Troubleshooting* tab in ME, check the option *Disable System Restore*. Virus scanners can now perform their tasks without restrictions in Windows XP/ME.

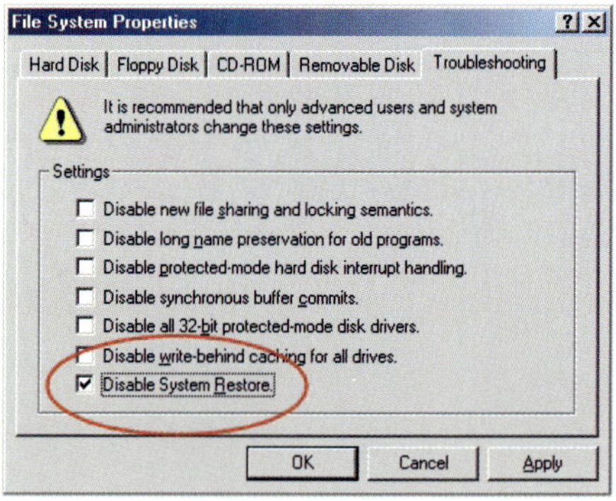

Only up-to-date virus information offers you real protection

The development of new viruses occurs incredibly fast. New mutants and appendages to disrupt your system appear almost weekly. Even if you have installed a virus scanner, it can only protect you from viruses known to it. From the moment you

5. Covering your tracks in the Internet

Do you know by any chance how many tracks you are leaving behind on the Web while you are innocently surfing from one site to the next? Each time you visit a Web site, your browser sends a deluge of information to the Web site's server: which site you are coming from, which browser you are using, which operating system you are using, your window size and a whole lot more. Using sophisticated statistics programs, an inference can be made about your surfing habits, and a visitor profile can be created. In addition, it probably isn't pleasant if the Web server of the operating system's manufacturer learns that you were visiting shady sites dedicated to illegal copying before switching to their site, for instance. If you even give your address or something similar because you are requesting information, a link to your identity is no longer a problem, and you can already imagine what the possible consequences are.

The Web site http://www.cyscape.com/showbrow.asp?all=1&bhcp=1 gives you an impressive demonstration of how much information can be gathered just by visiting a simple Web site.

Surfing anonymously

The "transparent" surfer has become a reality by now. He is no longer a piece of science fiction. Although data protectionists are still despairing about how much information is freely accessible, they too are required to protect their own privacy.

How you are identified: IPs and MACs

For a connection to a network such as the Internet, which is built on the TCP/IP protocol, you require a meaningful worldwide address - the IP address, referred to as IP for short. With this IP, the computer is unambiguously identifiable. If you are not exactly using a dedicated line, your IP is normally assigned dynamically for each session by your provider, so that each time a connection is made, a different one is drawn from the provider's pool of possibilities.

Because of this address, all your actions are linked to your computer, for, whenever you request a Web site, the router (intermediary computer) has to know where the data should be sent. In case of a legal action, for example, your provider's logs quickly provide information about who was assigned what IP and when. This way, any action can be quickly traced back to the computer of the person searched for.

If your IP is known to a hacker (this can be found out by simple trial and error, for instance), he can focus his attack on your computer. The longer your IP is active at any one time, the more time and chances of success he has.

> **Note**
>
> **Make life difficult for hackers**
>
> Avoid extremely long sessions (particularly with flat rates) and rather dial in anew more often. This only takes a couple of seconds, in exchange for which you are assigned a new IP address, which makes you more difficult to locate by hackers.

The IP you have just been assigned can be easily determined:

1 In Windows NT/2000/XP, open a window with the command prompt. Otherwise, go to *Start/Run* (Windows 98 depicted here).

2 In the *Run* dialog window, enter "winipcfg" (or "ipconfig" in at the command prompt for Windows NT/2000/XP).

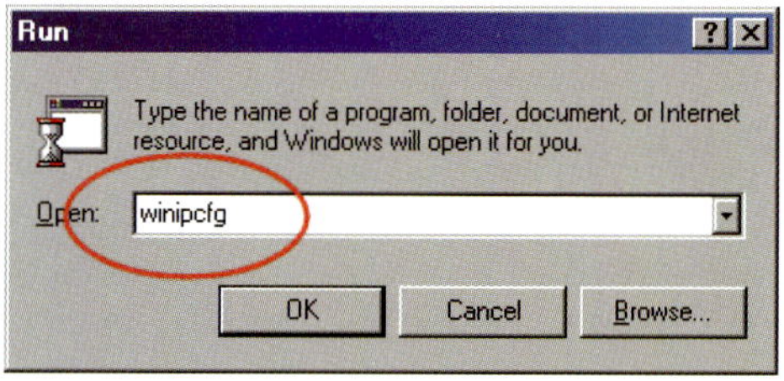

3 If you are not using Windows NT/2000/XP, the above window appears; in NT/2000/XP, the information is listed in the DOS window. If the above window appears and you have several network components, first select *PPP Adapter* in the *IP Configuration* to see the addresses for the dial-up network adapter. As soon as you go online and an IP address is dynamically assigned to you, the corresponding information is displayed.

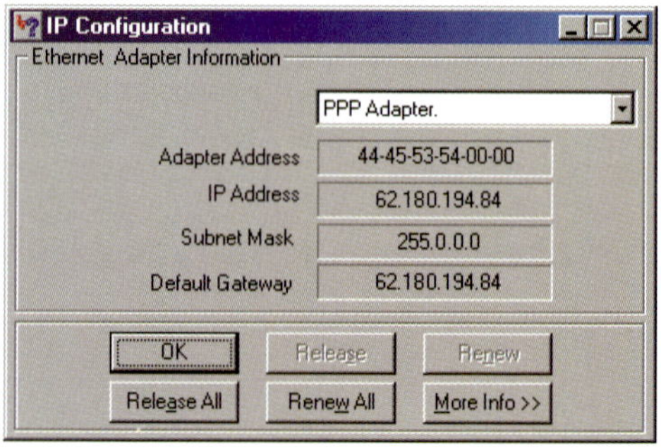

> **Note**
>
> **IP addresses and NetMeeting**
>
> The information about your IP address can also be used in other programs, for example, NetMeeting, to give a discussion participant the possibility to dial you up directly over the address, once you have disclosed this information.

Besides the IP address, which you can change each time you dial in anew, a second address unambiguously identifies your computer and does not change: the MAC address (**M**edium **A**ccess **C**ontrol) is a more permanent integral part of every network and ISDN card. The MAC address is always needed, regardless of which transport protocol (for example, TCP/IP) you are currently using, for network cards to exchange data with each other.

The card's manufacturer programs a globally unique address into each card.

Because a modem does not use a MAC address, Windows creates an additional address for such devices during installation, which, likewise, has a high possibility of being unique.

Even though the IP address still changes each time you dial in anew to your provider, the MAC address remains unique and this way makes it possible to make an unambiguous identification of your computer (or at least your network card, which is built into the computer) - in other words, an excellent starting point for illegal actions.

You can find the MAC address in the *IP Configuration* as well (see above). Look for the 6-byte *Adapter Address*.

Anonymizers offer protection

As you can see, you always leave tracks behind in the Web. To enjoy as much privacy as possible, it is therefore best to use a proxy server. Proxies take on an intermediary role between your provider and the Web host: If you want to see a Web site, ask the proxy to acquire it and pass it on to you. The Web site is then only connected to the proxy server and no longer directly to you. You can find out by contacting your provider if it maintains a proxy server and how you have to configure your Web browser. Unfortunately, the proxy still passes on some data to the

Web server, which allows for some inferences about your provider, so that you have not reached the optimal level of anonymity.

If your provider doesn't offer a proxy server, or you want to remain completely anonymous, only an anonymizer helps. These services filter out all the information when you request a Web site, and this way ensure complete protection. The disadvantage of such services is only that, in general, they work relatively slowly because all requests must pass through the anonymizer's computer. In addition, they are often costly or financed through advertising.

1 One of the best-known anonymizers is www.anonymizer.com.

2 To surf anonymously, all you have to do is enter the address of the desired Web site on the anonymizer's Web site.

3 When you use the anonymizer, advertising appears in the upper half of the target site. You can recognize the URL of the target site behind the information for the anonymizer.

Note

Monitoring in the workplace

Do you also like surfing at work during your breaks? Then, you must be particularly careful, for your employer could disapprove of this and take note of your activities, or even use them as a reason for firing you. You can find more information about this on page 132.

Here is where the information from the Net is saved on your hard drive

Dangers are not only lurking on the Web, but also on your hard drive where this or that information is saved, which can lead to your doom. Whenever you surf, complete directories full of the information about the Web sites you have visited are saved, and it is then easy to tell where you've been hanging out. At home, perhaps, this might only affect you and those you live with, but how would it look at your workplace?

There are basically four main groups to which the information saved by your browser belongs:

- **Cookies** are the best-known trespassers that are not deployed by the browser itself, but on behalf of the respective Web sites.
- The **History** provides information about when you visited what Web site. The browser automatically saves this information, with the main purpose of making navigation more convenient.
- In the **Cache**, all contents, such as images, text, and so forth of the visited Web sites are deposited. Depending on how large the cache is allowed to become, you can find the complete Web sites from the last few days. The data in the cache is used to display previously visited Web sites more quickly; the data doesn't then need to be loaded from the Web again, but can be quickly acquired from the hard drive.
- You yourself create **Bookmarks** to make life easier, so that you don't have to remember every URL.

Where you can find the relevant data and how you can delete it depends on the browser you are using. For you to clean up right away, the functions native to Netscape and Internet Explorer are now explained.

How Internet Explorer goes about saving

Unfortunately, it is not quite as easy to master data with Internet Explorer as it is with Netscape, because Microsoft has built in several back doors and, under Windows ME, the computer is protected from the operator so that only tricks help, for which you must first properly configure Windows Explorer:

1 Start Windows Explorer by going to *Start/Programs/Accessories/Windows Explorer*.

2 Go to the *Tools/Folder Options* command and switch to the *View* tab.

3 To get a maximum overview of your system and to uncover all its secrets, select the following settings:

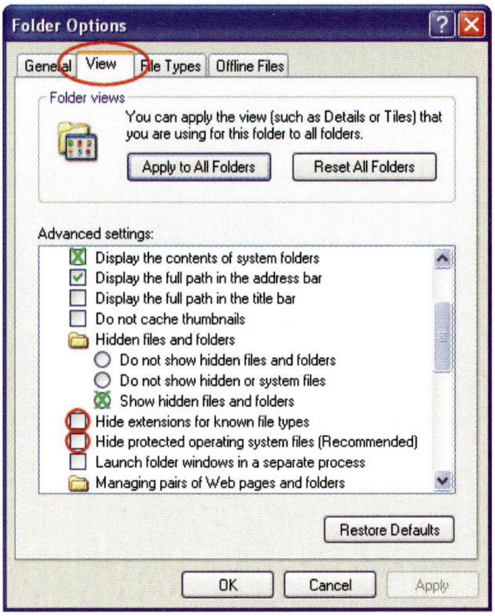

Option	Setting
Display the contents of system folders	on
Hide extensions for known file types	off
Hide protected operating system files	off
Show hidden files and folders	on

In Internet Explorer, cookies belong to the most obstinate of trespassers, as they are well protected by the system. They also take away a considerable amount of space, for each cookie is saved as its own file. Therefore, you can't pull any punches if you want to delete old cookies. These next steps apply in particular to Windows 95/98/Me running versions of Internet Explorer older than 6 (XP already includes the latest version of Internet Explorer).

5. Covering your tracks in the Internet

1 Start Windows Explorer by going to *Start/Programs/Accessories/Windows Explorer*.

2 Switch to the *C:\Documents and Settings*\User name\ directory and search in the *Cookies* folder.

3 All saved cookies are listed in the right window. To see the contents of one of the cookies, you can double-click the file to open it in the text editor.

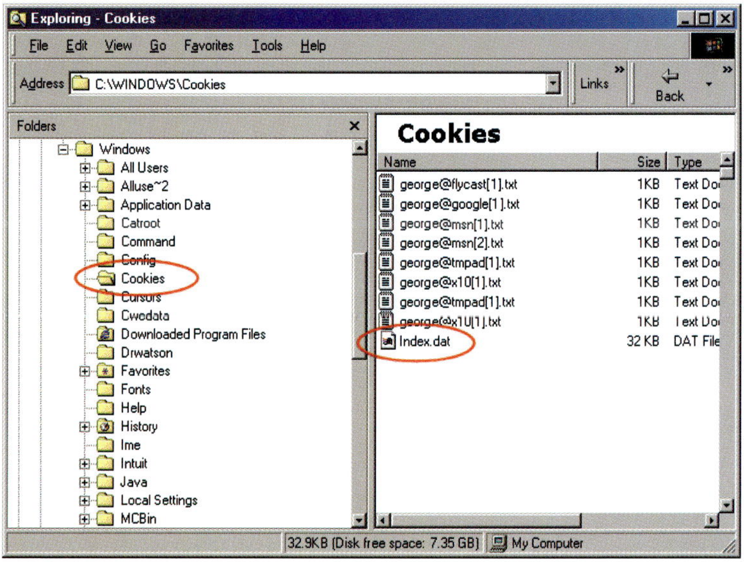

4 To delete the cookies, it would suffice to delete all of the text files. Annoyingly, the text files are just a sham, for all the cookies are additionally hidden in the *Index.dat* file, which is also visible. Because you are dealing with a system file, it cannot be deleted so easily.

5 Again click the Cookies folder and press [F2] or select *File/Rename*, to change the name of the folder. Rename the folder to anything you like (for example, *Cookies~*), press the [Enter] key, and acknowledge the prompt.

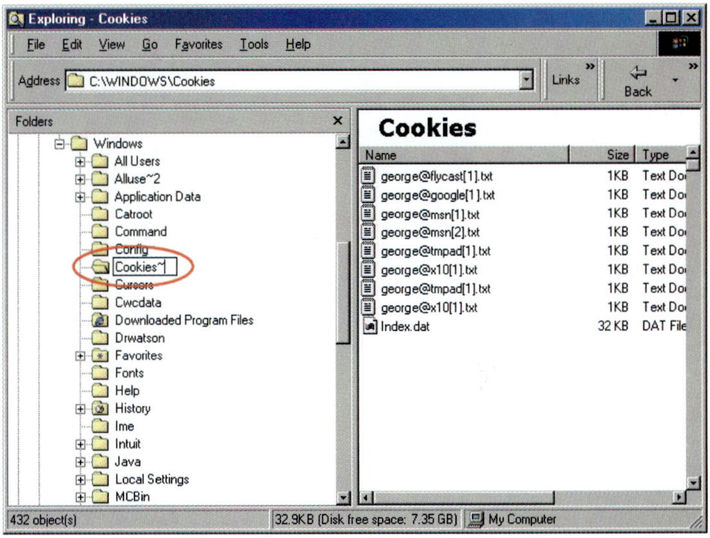

6 Click the *Windows* folder icon and create a new folder by going to *File/New/Folder*, which you must call *Cookies*.

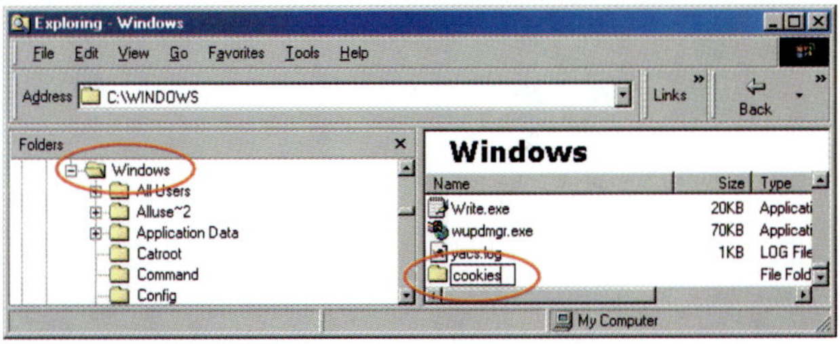

7 Incredibly, Windows still has a hand in it and would like to continue working with the original folder – regardless of what you have named it. Therefore, an excursion to the registry is in order. To get there, go to *Start/Run* and open the registry editor by entering "regedit".

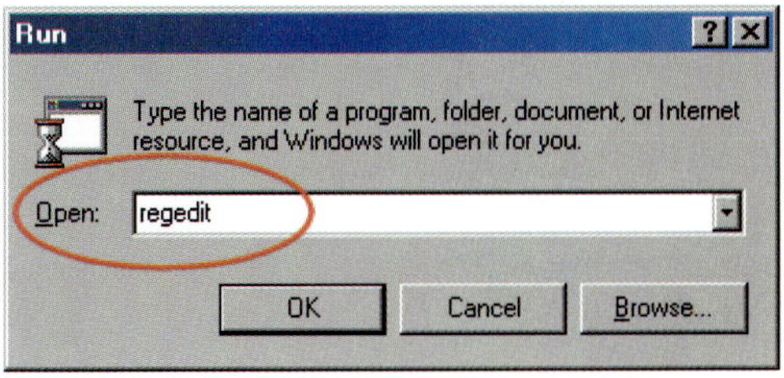

8 Look for the key *HKEY_CURRENT_USER\Software\Microsoft\Windows\CurrentVersion\Explorer\User Shell Folders*. In the right half of the window, you can then see the entry Cookies with the path to the original cookie folder.

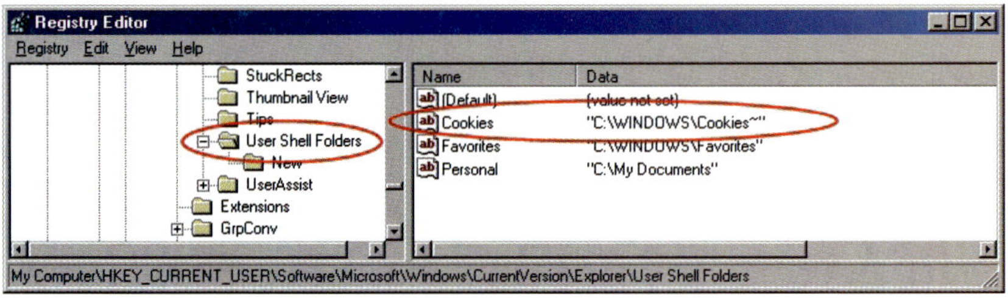

9 Double-click the Cookies entry and enter the path to the new cookie folder: "C:\Documents and Settings\User name\cookies".

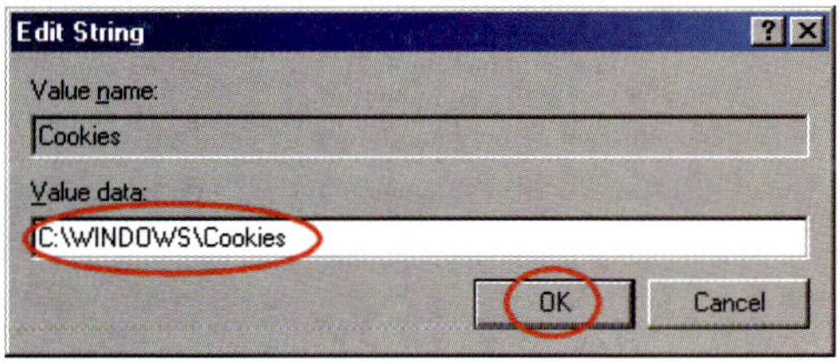

10 After you have rebooted your computer or have logged off and back on, Windows uses the new folder, creates a new Index.dat file and saves all future cookies here. You can now confidently delete the old folder.

Only as of Internet Explorer 6 can you conveniently delete cookies without having to fool around:

1 In Internet Explorer, select the menu item *Tools/Internet Options*.

2 You can delete all the cookies on the hard drive by clicking *Delete Cookies* in the *General* tab.

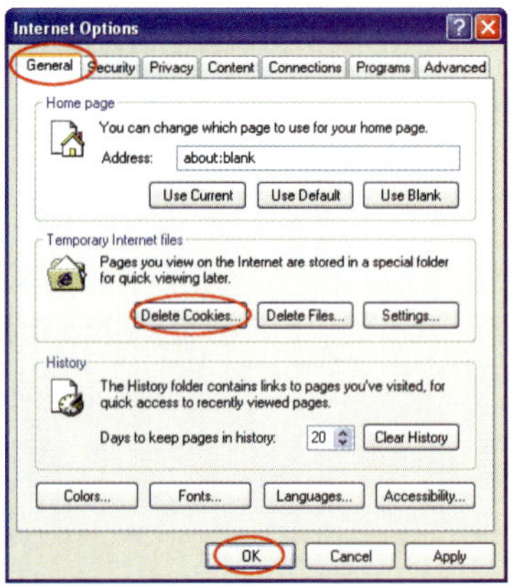

Internet Explorer manages the Web sites you visited in a folder called *History* and gives exact information on when you were where, which structures the time frames and Web sites into separate subfolders.

1 In Internet Explorer, select the menu item *Tools/Internet Options*.

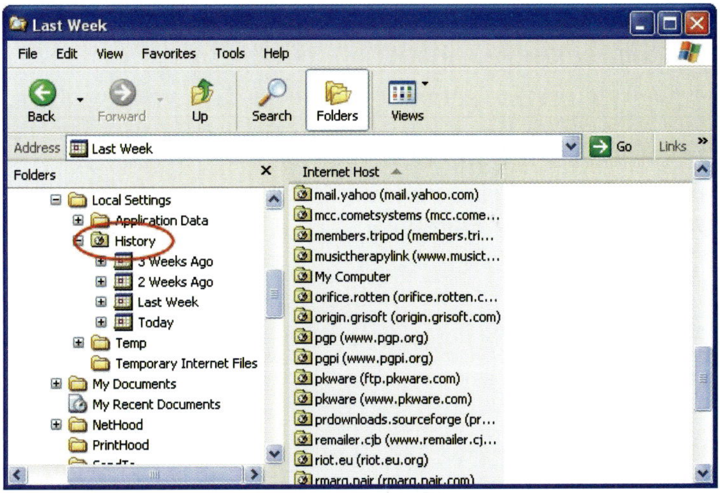

2 By clicking *Clear History* in the *General* tab, you can delete all the entries in the *History* folder and once again establish your privacy.

3 To accumulate less data during further tours of the Web, you can set the number of *Days to keep pages in history*. In contrast to Netscape, a value of *0* does not mean that nothing is recorded, but merely that only the current day is recorded.

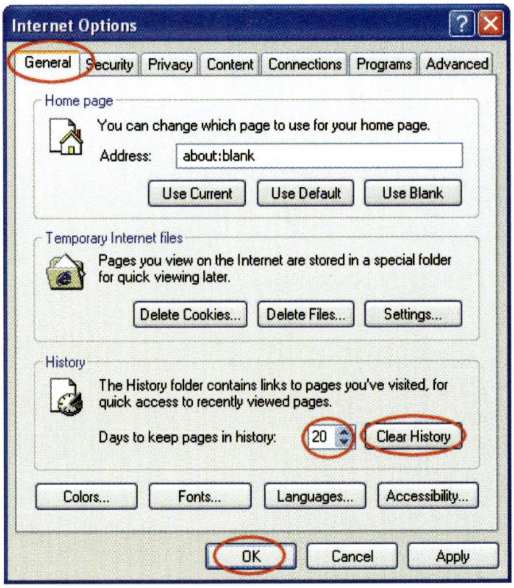

5. Covering your tracks in the Internet

Because the hard drive cache discloses information about the Web sites you have visited with Internet Explorer, it makes sense to clear it at times:

1 In Internet Explorer, go to the menu item *Tools/Internet Options*.

2 Click *Delete Files* to remove all the temporary cache files from your hard drive. Alternatively, you could also remove the contents of the folder *C:\Windows\Temporary Internet \Files* if you are using 98/Me, or *C:\Documents and Settings*\User name\ *Local Settings\Temporary Internet Files* if you are using 2000/XP, in Explorer.

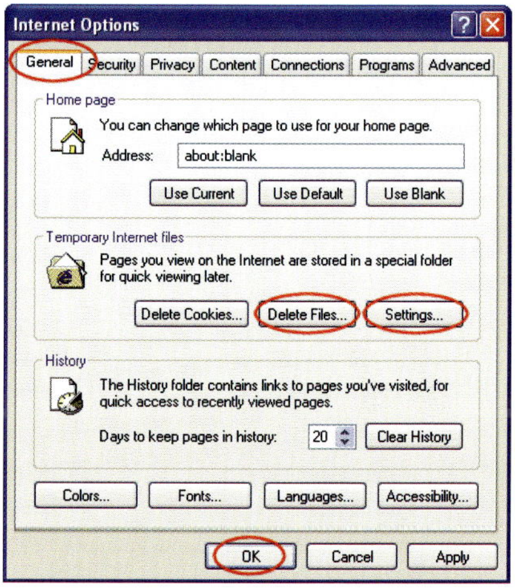

3 You can reach the settings for setting the size of the cache through *Settings*. With the slider or the arrow symbols next to the amount of disk space to use, you can determine the maximum available hard drive space in MB. You can unfortunately not completely turn off the cache - 1 MB is namely the smallest possible setting.

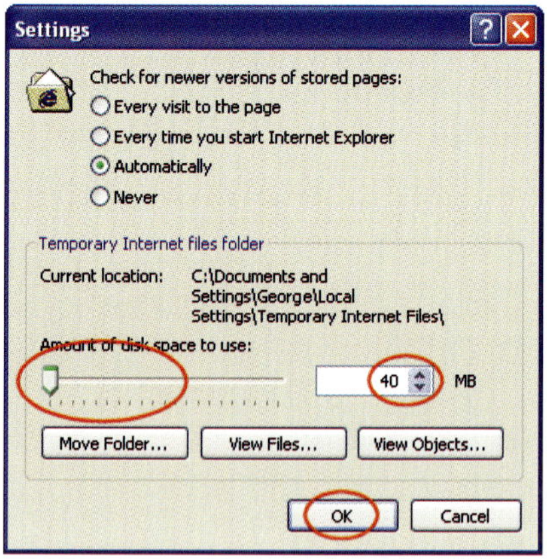

Bookmarks in Internet Explorer - called Favorites - can be organized by going to *Favorites/Organize Favorites* in the menu. Afterwards, they can be deleted in order not to leave behind any tell-tale traces of the sites you find interesting.

1 Open the *Organize Favorites* dialog window and search for the entry you want to edit. You can open and then close folders by double-clicking them.

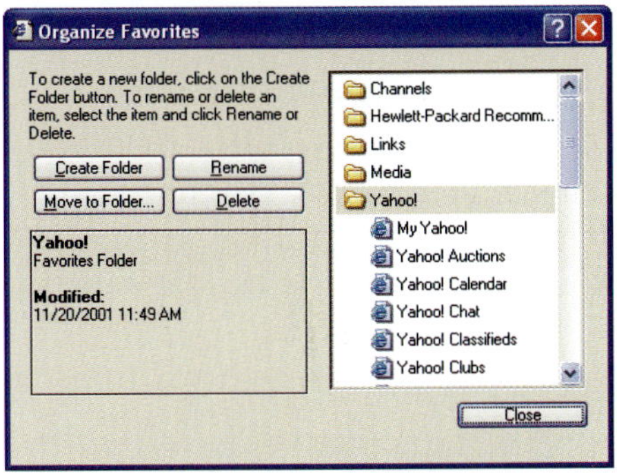

2 You can delete a single entry or an entire folder and all the bookmarks it contains by selecting the current entry and then pressing on [Delete] or by clicking *Delete*.

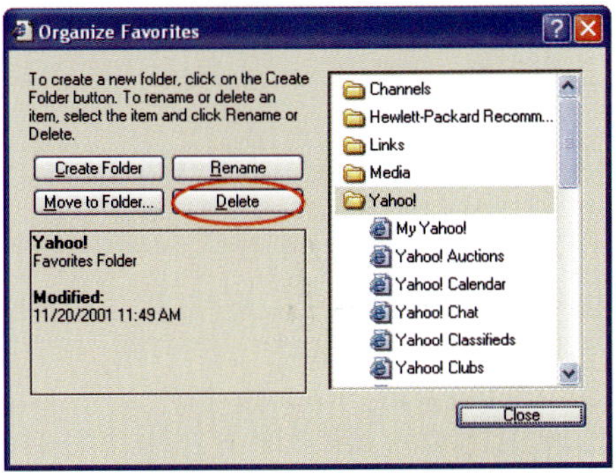

3 You have quite convenient access to a large number of deletion functions in Explorer, because you can immediately select several entries there without having to confirm the deletion for each one. The folder *C:\Documents and Settings*\User name*Favorites* (XP and Me; *C:\Windows\Favorites* in 98/ME)

contains the exact same entries as the Favorites dialog window. Because we are dealing with a completely normal folder and files, you can select the files in Explorer the way you normally would and delete them with the Delete key.

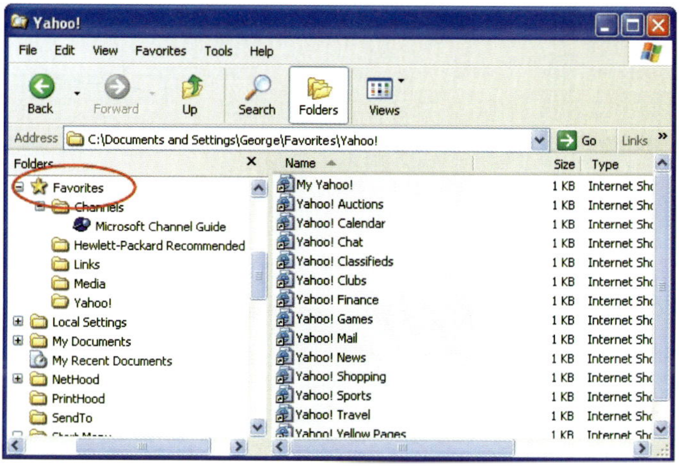

Big Brother is watching you

In 1948, Orwell wrote the classic *1984*. A good 50 years later, no one doubts the idea of a transparent, completely monitored mankind. Network engineering has met all the technical requirements, from an organizational viewpoint, to make controlling coworkers at every turn possible and to monitor, log, and evaluate all their activities and then, as a final consequence, to admonish those who have stepped outside the established rules, firing them upon repetition.

From the point of view of those who are accountable, there are naturally a number of reasons for monitoring, for example:

- Unrelated surfing during work time burdens the bandwidth, costs money, and hinders other employees from proceeding with their work. In addition, stronger viruses and other harmful programs could be introduced.
- The same goes for personal mail. It is always possible that company secrets are revealed this way.

- Other colleagues could feel harassed by the Web sites visited (for example, by pornographic material).
- The download of a number of programs could be illegal and could cost bandwidth for access to the network. By the (short-term) saving of data, the company also becomes liable.

For these reasons, it is not uncommon for the employment contract or company policy to state what is and isn't allowable for employees and in what context. Finally, few employers are interested in seeing the work lying around while the employees are playing shoot 'em up games on the Web or looking for the latest pirated software.

As the system administrator of a company network, it is absolutely no problem, from a technical point of view, to be precisely informed about all the network access activities and to keep logs. Almost always, this data more or less falls by the wayside as the waste product of completely routine maintenance or use, for most programs deposit a lot of information on the hard drive (see page 123). The server software, which keeps the internal working of the network organized and running in the background, additionally saves further information, from which surfing profiles can be created and can, for example, be used to assign the data volume used by individual users. Users with a consistently high volume of data flow (as experienced with file downloads, for instance) are naturally detected right away.

Various manufacturers have in the meantime recognized that, in addition to company management, there is a large interest in sniffing programs. Network Associates offers Sniffer (http://www.sniffer.com), a program that logs the data traffic bit for bit in a network. This way, not only undesirable sojourns on the Web can be detected, but passwords can also be spied out, and the entire data traffic saved for evidence, and so forth.

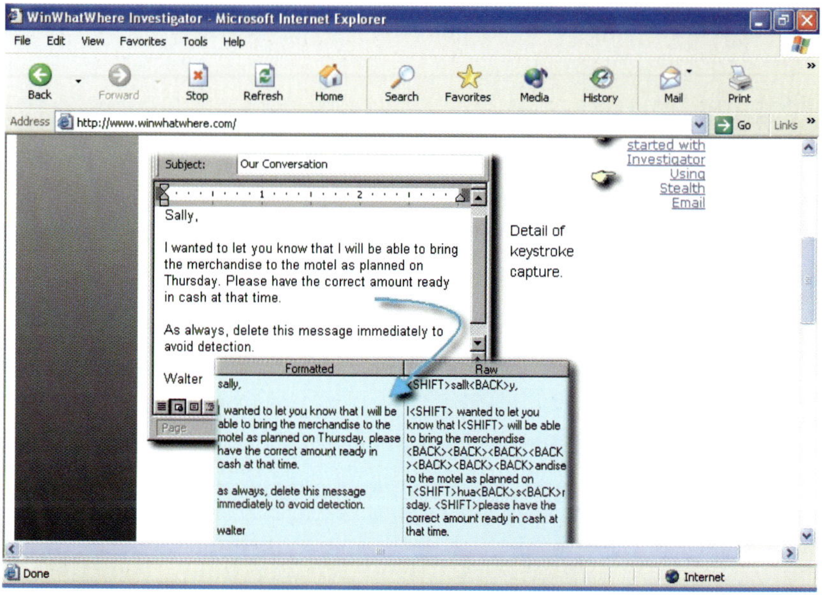

http://www.winwhatwhere.com

The software WinWhatWhere (http://www.winwhatwhere.com) even goes a step further and virtually looks over the user's shoulder. Not only do all the network activities land in a log file, but every mouse click and key stroke, the time that has passed between two actions, and even where the mouse was moved to, is saved and logged. Goodbye to privacy.

The extent to which such a type of complete monitoring is actually permissible has to be regulated in the employment contract and be clarified with the workers' committee (if one is available). E-mails, for the most part, fall under the subject of letter privacy and cannot be simply read by the employer, unless they are business related. Business e-mails, in contrast, can be looked at, and, if the company prohibits the use of private e-mails, all e-mail traffic can be viewed from a business standpoint. If a private e-mail is contained within, tough luck for the writer - unless it is expressly marked as private, in which case, you care going against the stipulations.

6. Hide your data behind a protective Internet wall

Because your computer is a potential target the minute it connects to the Internet and you can rarely keep up-to-date with all the possible dangers, you need an effective protective mechanism to guard you and your data as well as possible from current Trojan horses, spyware, script kiddies, and so on.

In the building industry, you can get protection from overall dangers through firewalls: should a part of the building catch fire, it can't spread to the neighboring complexes if a solid wall is standing between them.

Such firewalls are also available for computers and networks. And if you have saved confidential information on your computer, or you simply just have something against unauthorized access and spying on information, then firewalls offer excellent protection, so that your stay in the Web does not lead to paranoia and you can once again surf in peace.

How a firewall can protect you

Until recently, firewalls were something with which only system administrators of large companies had to and could grapple. Technology has in the meantime changed so much that no computer owner who surfs the Internet can actually get by without one, for increasingly more people are particularly bent on causing harm to others.

A firewall works on a simple principle: the program positions itself between the computer and the Internet and simply blocks the entire exchange of data. This way, no attacks can be made on the computer and no information can be extracted.

6. Hide your data behind a protective Internet wall

This radical solution doesn't make sense, however, because you cannot exchange information with the Internet and thus create a connection. For this reason, a firewall has to be configured in such a way as to intercept most of the data at least once, but also permit some to pass through.

To accomplish this, the firewall eavesdrops on all connections (the ports) between the computer and the network. If an application that is allowed to send information to the Net tries to do so, the action takes place. However, if an application that does not have permission tries to send information, the information gets intercepted and a warning message appears in most cases, which tells you who wants to communicate.

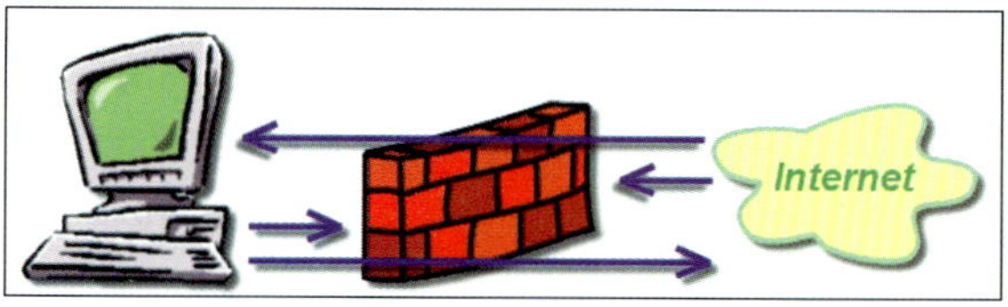

Similarly, a firewall protects you from data on the Net: if data packets that were requested arrive and are targeted at a permissible application, they are allowed. All other attempts to pass through to the computer fail, whereby you can likewise become informed about it so that you can recognize and respond to possible attacks accordingly.

Note

Firewalls offer all-around protection

Firewalls not only help against attacks from the Internet. It can make sense to also use them on local networks, thereby making it possible to control all the data traffic between your computer and the network components.

In addition to protecting you from the large number of programs that were presented in the chapter about viruses and company starting on page 95 and which surreptitiously enjoy sending data into the Net, firewalls also offer protection from the popular port scans.

To conduct a port scan, the attacker runs a simple program on his computer to determine the IP address and then scours you PC for all possible connections, to see if an open connection exists perchance.

Attacks can then be started from such a port. Depending on which port is open, the attacker can run programs on your computer or gather information from it. Without a firewall, you are left clueless, until you start to wonder why your PC is missing information or your account statements have been made public on the Web.

On the Shields Up Web site, you can trigger such an attack on your computer and determine which ports present a security risk at present.

1 Begin the test by going to the Web site https://grc.com/x/ne.dll?bh0bkyd2. You can start the self-attempt with. *Probe My Ports*.

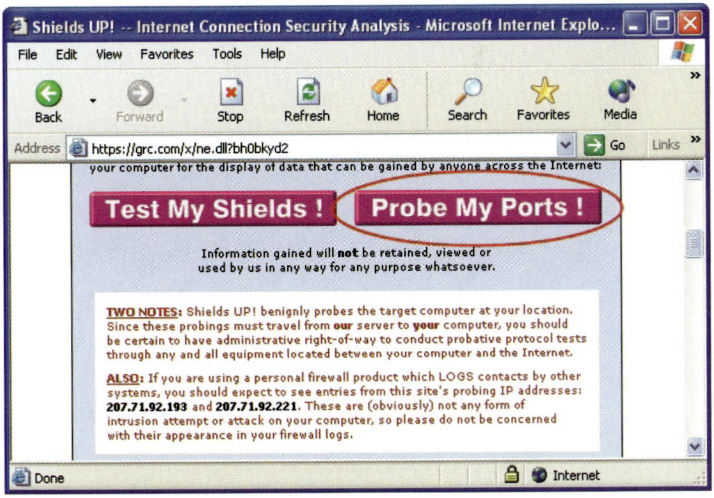

2 After the test, you see a report in which all the open ports are listed. Depending on which protocols are active at that port, different dangers present themselves.

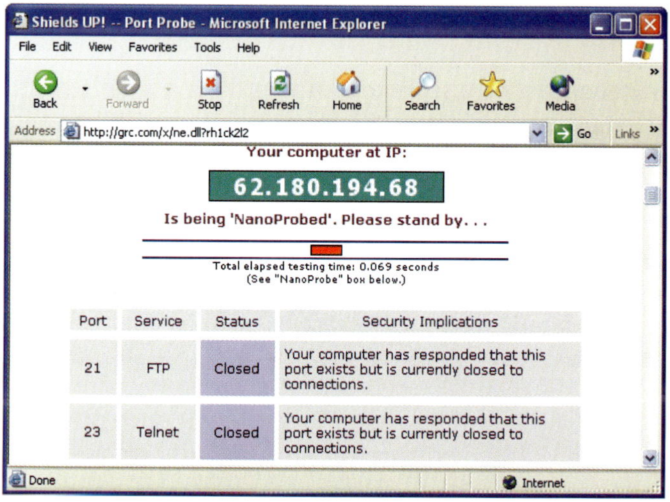

Installing a free firewall

You can choose from a vast number of firewalls, ranging from free to expensive and from incomprehensible to user-friendly. One of the most popular firewall programs for private users combines two prominent advantages: it's free and user-friendly. Thus, nothing stops you from installing it immediately, so you can once again surf in peace.

At http://www.zonelabs.com, the Web site for ZoneAlarm, you can download the approximately 2-MB file free of charge (you only require the Pro version if you are using the program professionally).

1 Start the setup program after downloading by double-clicking the file name in Explorerclicking.

2 Read the information contained in the first two dialog fields and then give your name, and so forth in the text entry fields. If you register with ZoneAlarm, you receive information through e-mail and automatic updates, which you can, however, get yourself.

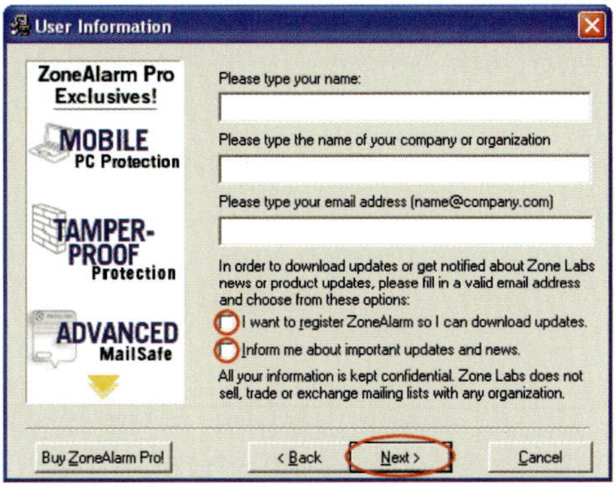

3 Accept the license agreement and, in the next step, select the installation path with *Browse* or use the one recommended.

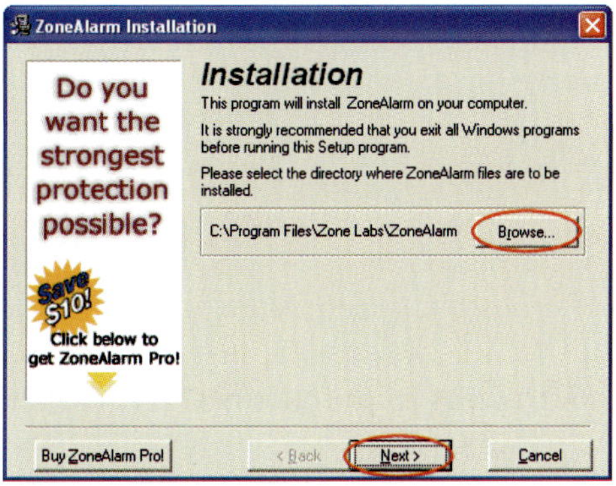

4 After installation, some user information is requested, of which the most important to select is *Personal Use*.

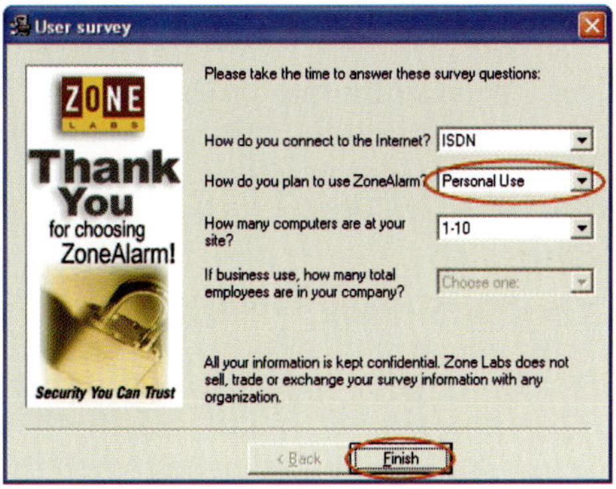

5 Once you have completed the steps, you must restart the computer, so that your personal firewall can become active, which you can recognize by the appearance of the icon in the system tray.

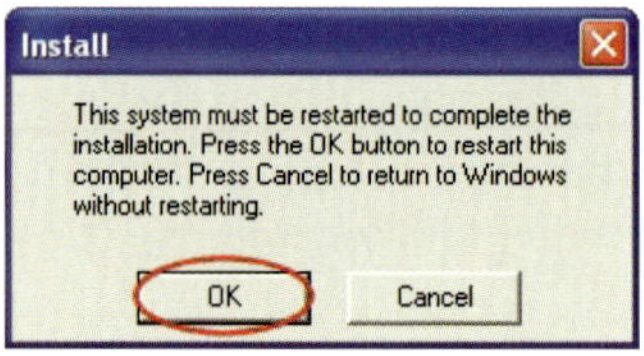

Note

Data transfer always under control

With the help of the two bar graph displays in the ZoneAlarm icon, you can always have an overview over whether data is currently being sent to the Net (red) or being received (green). The higher the display reaches, the higher the transfer rate.

Everyday surfing with the firewall

After installing ZoneAlarm, all access to and from the network is initially blocked 100%. This way, you ensure the highest degree of security, but you can no longer have access to the Internet. You must therefore configure the firewall somewhat to allow several programs to still communicate with the Internet.

Note

Even your local network is affected

If you have several computers at home that you have networked for multi-player games, for example, these computers are initially locked out by ZoneAlarm. The Help explains how you can assign rights for networks. If you don't have an active Internet connection, you can also close the firewall by right clicking the icon (*Shutdown ZoneAlarm*).

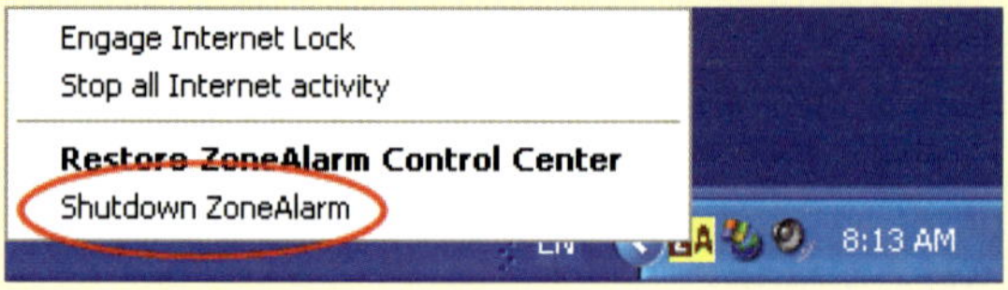

Determining access rights for programs

As soon as you want to use a program to access a network, ZoneAlarm registers this request and knows if the program is entitled to do so or not.

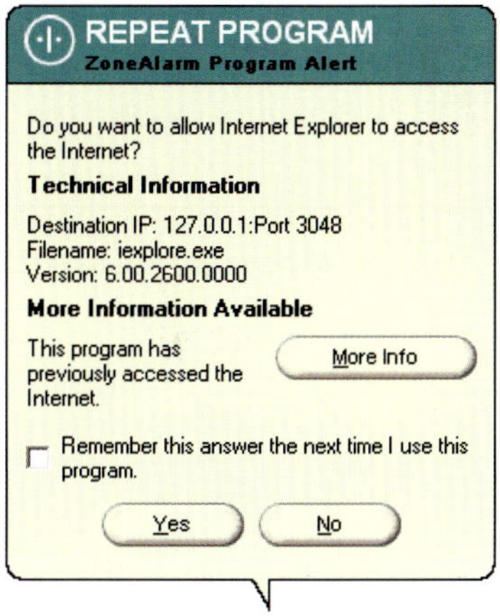

1 As soon as an application wants to send information, a warning message appears, informing you about the access. Carefully read through the information, for it could be dealing with a program that has absolutely no right to have access to the Net and wants to send private information.

2 If you want to grant access for the program (here: Internet Explorer) to the Internet, click *Yes,* otherwise, *No*.

3 ZoneAlarm can remember your decision, which is convenient for several standard applications that can otherwise annoy you with each new access. If you enable the *Remember the answer each time* option, the firewall remembers if you have clicked *Yes* or *No*, and automatically uses the selection in the future.

Because no rights have been set in any way at the beginning, you have a lot more prompts than usual in the first few days, until you have determined the settings for all the programs.

Note

Assigning rights conservatively

You should be very stingy with permitting access rights to the Internet. Many programs would love to send information into the Internet, but they don't actually need to. Your browser and e-mail programs definitely are entitled to permanent access; and programs such as TSAdBot definitely are not. Then there are still a large number of programs in whose case it is better for you to decide anew each time. This is, for example, the case with Media Player, which needs to have access to the Internet when it requires new drivers or something similar, but which also likes to send out information about you. Even if the prompts by ZoneAlarm cost you some time, you can in this way increase your security. Do not just give permission across the board, but first look when and which program wants to communicate with the Internet.

6. Hide your data behind a protective Internet wall

If you want to correct some decisions you have made or generally determine which programs have what rights, ZoneAlarm makes it possible through a simple dialog window:

1 Open ZoneAlarm's configuration window by double-clicking the program icon in the system tray.

2 Click *Programs* to see all the programs that are currently registered in ZoneAlarm. In the *Allow connect column*, you can see the rights of the respective programs for the local network and the Internet. The symbols have the following meanings:

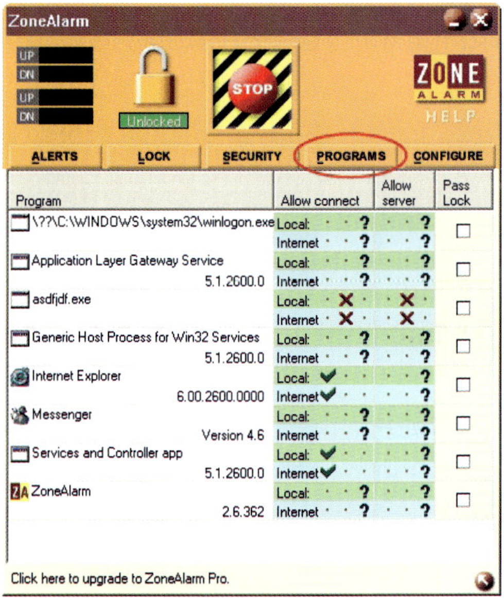

Symbol	Term	Meaning for the program
	Ask	You are prompted for each new access attempt.
	Allow	Data can always be exchanged.
	Disallow	No data can be exchanged.

3 You can change the rights at any time by right-clicking a program entry and selecting the new settings in the context menu. With *Remove*, you also have the option of deleting the program from the list, for instance, if you have completely uninstalled it.

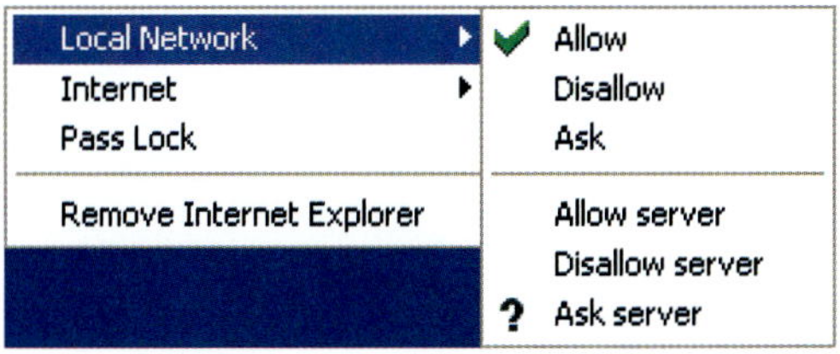

Non-stop attacks? – Don't panic!

ZoneAlarm not only controls the data that is being sent from your computer to the network, but also that which is being received. Should a hacker try to take action against you while you are online, for example, the firewall is effectively in the way.

With an installed firewall, you can also have good protection against bugs in programs that are not yet well known or for which no solutions exist, as, for example, the hole in Microsoft NetMeeting. This hole allows the attacker to saturate the victim's computer 100% by means of a Denial-of-service attack, making working with the computer impossible. With a firewall, you are protected against such activities.

In the illustration, a user from heart.newyork.com with IP address *141.64.3.216* is trying to obtain access to your computer through telnet, which would be prevented by ZoneAlarm.

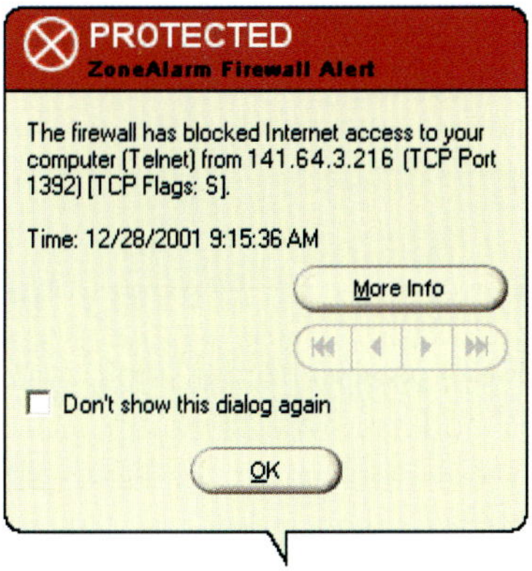

For each potential attack attempt, ZoneAlarm displays a notification containing detailed information about which service just tried to access your computer and from where. Thus, you have the opportunity to determine if you are dealing with a real threat. For more information, you can click *More info*, which connects you to ZoneAlarm's Web site.

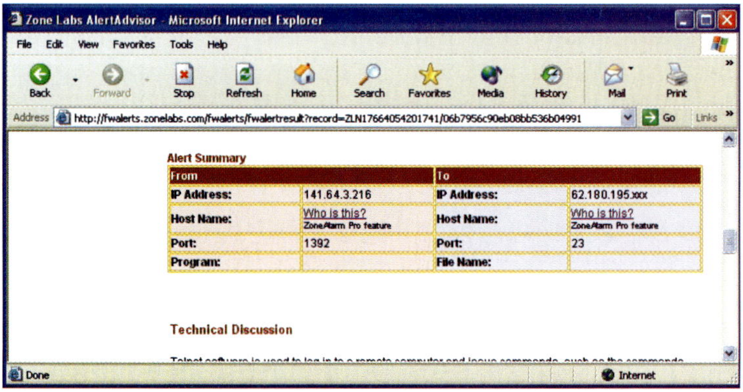

http://fwalerts.zonelabs.com

One of the characteristics of firewalls that you might likely encounter is that they send innumerable warnings after you have closed a session with a Web site (for example, by ending the session and shortly thereafter creating a new connection).

This occurs because the original Web site is still sending information, but it is not being addressed to the correct port used during the first session. Fortunately no real dangers occur from these types of data packets, but the error messages can get on your nerves after a while. Suppress them with the *Don't show this dialog again* option.

How to catch every hacker

If the attacks from a single system - which you can recognize from the unchanged IP address - are piling up, you can also take up arms and act against the alleged hacker, for, even if she is not doing any damage to you, because you are protected by a firewall, other users might have worse luck, if a hacker continues to be a nuisance.

Because you cannot discover who the hacker is directly - after all, she'll hardly give her name and also rarely be the owner of the IP address from which she is undertaking the attack (that would be too simple and you would be dealing with an exceptionally stupid hacker) - you can only get in contact with the computer's system administrator from where the attack originated. Inform yourself as much as possible about the attack on your system. With concrete information, the administrator can then take a look at the log files and most likely identify the hacker. Because a system administrator can hardly sympathize with the hacker, the administrator is already motivated and wants to bring about the relevant legal action. If that is not enough, you can always consider initiating your own legal procedure.

In any case, you must be sure of the following information and approach the administrator with it:

- the time of the attack (to the second) and the date
- the type of attack (for example, telnet, ping, and so forth)
- the IP address and port from which the attack came

As you can see, this is the exact information that ZoneAlarm provides you with in the warning message; all you have to do is write it down. Additionally, a screenshot wouldn't hurt. To take one, press the [PrintScreen] key and paste the image from the Clipboard into a graphics program; then save it.

Once you have secured the "evidence", all you need to do is find out who is responsible for the system the attacker used. To find out, it is best to click *More info* in the warning message to get to the ZoneLabs Web site, as previously described.

1 In the table (see above), you can click *Who is this* (Professional version only) in the *Source* column to determine the computer's proprietor; alternatively, you can also go to the ARIN Web site and manually begin your search.

2 A query is then made at the **A**merican **R**egistry for **I**nternet **N**umbers organization (ARIN) (http://www.arin.net/whois). The search is either answered immediately, or ARIN gives a clue as to the administrators responsible for the IP address.

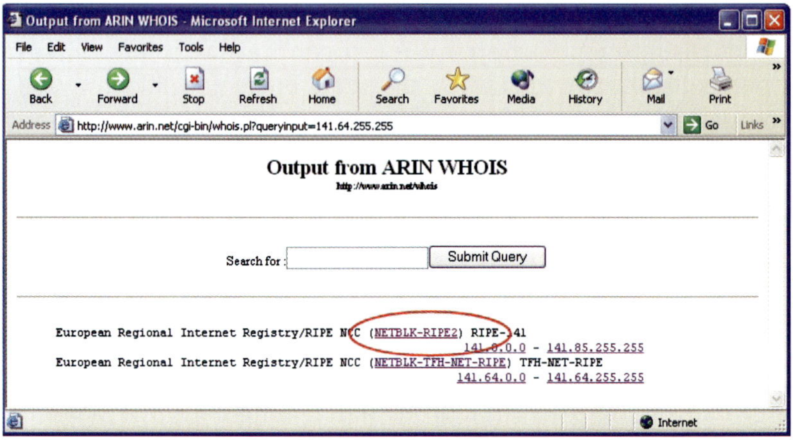

http://www.arin.net/whois

3 For European addresses, the equivalent site is RIPE (**R**éseaux **IP E**uropéens, http://www.ripe.net), whose URL is displayed if you click the links in ARIN's search results.

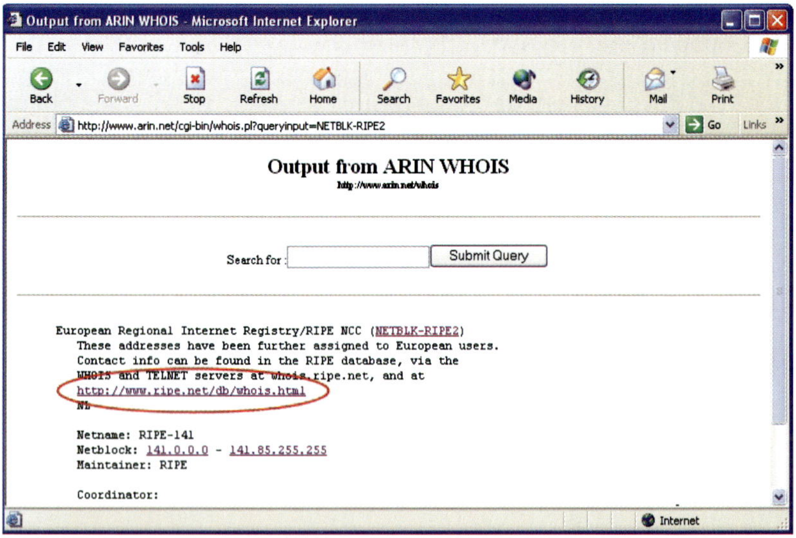

4 By entering the IP address into the search form of the specified administration (in this example, RIPE), you advance a step in your search for the system proprietor.

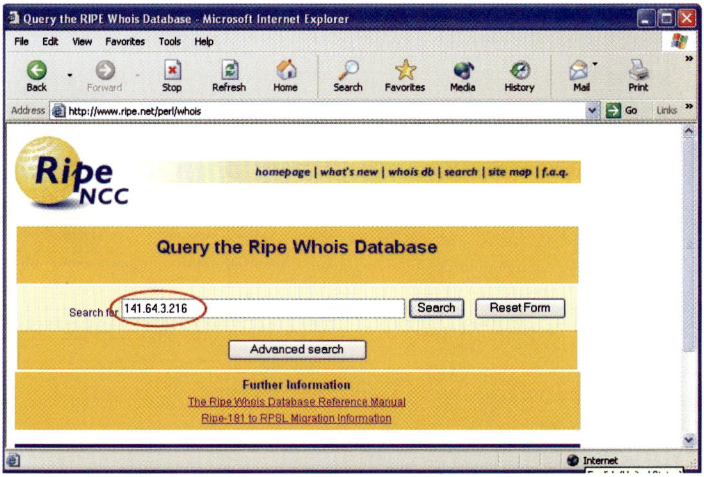

http://www.ripe.net/perl/whois

5 After a successful search, all the information saved in the database is then presented to you. Now you know who was entered as the owner of the attacking computer or, put more precisely, the net server behind which the attacker is hiding.

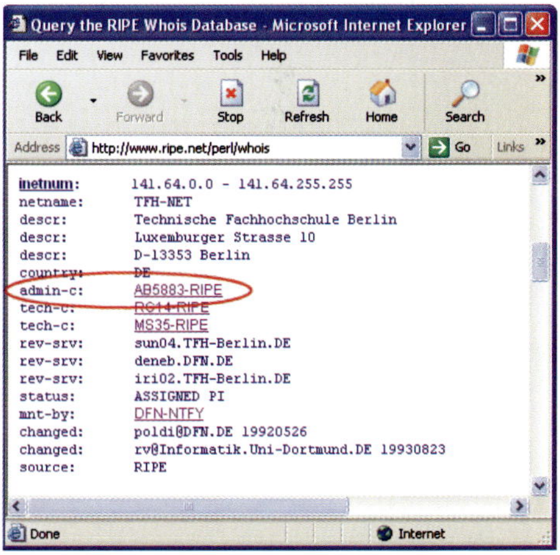

6 To find out the name and e-mail address of the administrator, you must click the link under *admin-c*; you now have all the information necessary to implicate the hacker.

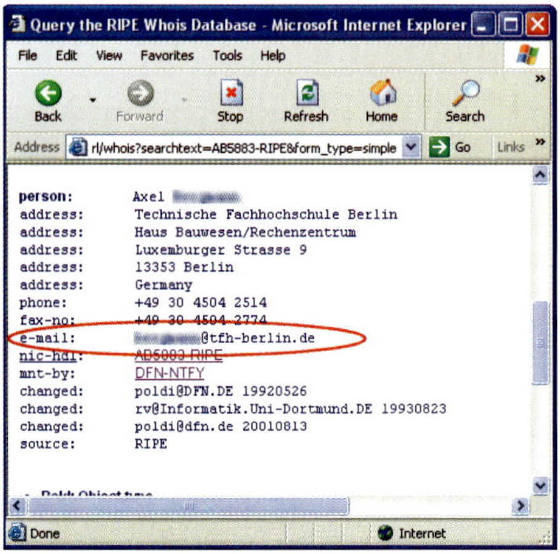

Index

A

B

C

D

E

F

W

Y

Z

Notes

Notes